C000279557

Wheelwrights to Wickets

THE STORY OF
THE CRICKETING HEARNES

Wheelwrights to Wickets

THE STORY OF
THE CRICKETING HEARNES

BY

J.W. "JACK" HEARNE

FOREWORD BY E.W. SWANTON

Boundary Books

To the memory of Herbert Royden Hearne
and to Luke, Andrew and Simon

Boundary Books Ltd
Southlands
Goostrey, Cheshire
CW4 8NT

All rights reserved. No part of this publication may be reproduced or transmitted in any form or by any means, electronic or mechanical, including photocopying, recording or any information storage and retrieval system now known or to be invented without permission in writing from the publisher.

First published 1996

This Edition ISBN 0 95 22070 60

Deluxe Edition ISBN 0 95 22070 79

©J.W. Hearne

Printed by Heathland Printers Ltd., Leek, Staffordshire
Bound by Hartnoll's of Bodmin

Contents

Chapter		Page
	FOREWORD by E.W. Swanton C.B.E.	4
	INTRODUCTION	7
1	THOMAS HEARNE – 'Old Tom'	11
2	THOMAS ARTHUR HEARNE	33
3	GEORGE FRANCIS HEARNE	37
4	THOMAS JOHN HEARNE	45
5	GEORGE HEARNE – 'Old George'	49
6	GEORGE GIBBONS HEARNE	59
7	FRANK HEARNE	70
8	ALEC HEARNE	83
9	RANDOLPH HEARNE	96
10	GEORGE ALFRED LAWRENCE HEARNE	100
11	HERBERT HEARNE	105
12	WALTER HEARNE	110
13	JOHN THOMAS HEARNE	116
14	JOHN WILLIAM HEARNE	133
15	WILLIAM HEARN(E)	158
16	SOME WILLIAM HEARNES	161
17	THE FAMILY	163
	ACKNOWLEDGEMENTS	165
	STATISTICAL APPENDIX	166
	INDEX	168
	A SELECTIVE FAMILY TREE	172

Foreword

by E.W. Swanton, C.B.E.

IT IS a pleasure to have been asked by John Wilfred Hearne to contribute a Foreword to his history of the great cricketing tribe of Hearne. Mr. Hearne is the son of John William, the greatest cricketer in the family, known throughout the sporting world as 'Young Jack', to differentiate him from his kinsman, the famous J.T., also named Jack.

The author, young Young Jack, so to say (though he is past the psalmist's span), was good enough to suggest that I was well qualified to undertake this task seeing that I have been identified with both Middlesex and Kent, between which counties the Hearnes divided their services. This is true in that though playing only a few times in the 1930s for Middlesex and for Middlesex 2nd XI I was fairly close to the side in those days through my friendship with Ian Peebles, while I have for many years been intimately concerned with the affairs of Kent.

It is half a century and more since J.W. last put on his pads for Middlesex and much longer since Alec, the most distinguished of the Kentish Hearnes, helped his county to win the first of its Championships. Yet the name remains an honoured one in both counties, and there are many with fond memories of one of the immortal partnerships in history, that of J.W. and Pat Hendren. (What a plethora of H's there were among the metropolitan counties for the Cockney paper-sellers to abbreviate in the days of my youth: 'obbs, 'itch, 'ayes, 'earne, 'endren, 'aig, 'ardinge, 'ubble – the entire cricket scene presided over with autocratic benevolence by their lordships of 'arris and 'awke!)

Middlesex and Kent boasted five Hearnes apiece, and between 1859 and 1936 there was never a year without a Hearne in the first-class averages, generally two or three. When J.T., prince of medium-pacers, began his 26-year career with Middlesex in 1888 brother Walter and cousins George, Frank and Alec were stalwart all-rounders for Kent.

Frank's son, G.A.L., although born in England, played and coached for Western Province and came with the South Africans to England to play in the Test series of 1924. There was a cousin of the Kentish brotherhood, G.F., who played a single match for MCC, as later did his son, T.J., who also made a single first-class appearance for Middlesex and did not even get to the wicket.

All in all, then, 13 Hearnes tested first-class cricket, a tally leaving them ahead of the field, well clear of the distinguished families of Lyttelton and Foster with nine apiece, Grace with eight, and Townsend with seven.

The mark made by the Hearnes on the Test scene derived chiefly from J.T., whose classic medium-pace, from a beautiful action earned him 49 wickets at 20 runs each in the 1890s, and from J.W. who, despite the loss of four prime years to the First World War and an in-and-out health record afterwards, was chosen for 24 Tests between 1911/12 and 1926. In early days Frank, George and Alec also toured South Africa, playing in what were subsequently considered Tests. Including the aforesaid G.A.L. the Hearne Test tally comes to six.

It was however chiefly as county cricketers and men of MCC that the family earned such renown and respect. Only three bowlers in history have bettered J.T.'s bag of 3,061 wickets. J.W. three times made 2,000 runs and took a hundred wickets: his full career figures were 37,352 runs (including 96 hundreds), average 40, and 1,839 wickets at 24 a time.

As for the earlier Kentish all-rounder Hearnes, Alec when he retired after the Championship year of 1906 had scored more runs for Kent and taken more wickets than any other man. His cousin Walter was reaching his peak as a bowler when a severe knee injury halted his career, after which he acted for many years as the county scorer.

The Hearnes indeed held a record of service to the game beyond the playing of it. For many years in term time J.T. coached at Oxford, as did J.W. post-war for Middlesex. Tom, the senior Hearne, was head groundsman at Lord's for more than 20 years, one son, young Tom, became Ground Superintendent and the other, G.F., Chief Clerk. Other Hearnes doubled with MCC as ground bowlers. G.F.'s service at Lord's lasted 46 years. It was the fact of "old George" Hearne being groundsman for the Private Banks at Catford Bridge, where in 1875, the first year of Lord Harris's captaincy, Kent played all their home matches, that established the Kent connection. In fact no Hearne was Kentish born. The family roots for centuries had lain in Buckinghamshire, recent generations having settled in Chalfont St.Giles and Chalfont St.Peter where they followed the craft of wheelwrights.

I had the privilege of knowing J.W., 'Young Jack', not well but sufficiently to appreciate his steadfast worth and quiet humour. Pat Hendren was the jovial Irish extrovert, the hero, well deserving of popular acclaim; but it was J.W. (as they always referred to him) who had a special place in the affections of his successive captains, Plum Warner, Frank Mann, Nigel Haig, Tom Enthoven and Walter Robins.

His character and disposition clearly mirrored those of his kinsmen. Of Thomas, the eldest of the cricketing Hearnes, *Wisden* recorded at his death in 1900 that "in personal character no professional cricketer stood higher, and all through his life he enjoyed the respect of everyone who knew him." Lord Harris wrote of his Hearne contemporaries as friends as well as comrades on the field. Alec was quiet of speech and manner, modest and, like all of them, being steeped in the game was an excellent judge of it. J.T. was the second professional cricketer, William Gunn of Notts being the first, to be elected to his county committee. Hubert Preston, editor of *Wisden*, concluded his tribute in the 1945 Almanack thus: "To be on friendly terms with J.T. for 50 years, as I was, meant an education in cricket and good fellowship."

The author, it seems to me, has gone about his task in the spirit of the Hearnes, conscientiously, thoroughly and I congratulate him warmly on the result. Even his father can never have played a more polished innings.

E.W. Swanton
Sandwich, January 1996

Introduction

THAT this book came to be written is due largely to chance, and to the continued encouragement of all those who have made such generous contributions to the text and illustrations.

A few years ago a writer requested information on my father's early years. After looking out material readily to hand and once again examining details of the Hearne family cricket eleven which appeared in the issue of *Cricket. A Weekly Record of the Game* for 9th May 1907, it came to mind that my father and grandfather had always asserted that we were related to all the men shown in the picture accompanying the article.

Until then, it must be frankly admitted that these and many other facts and figures concerning notable cricketing relatives had scarcely been given a second thought. For some reason, on this occasion it seemed a good idea to establish this relationship once and for all, but I had no intention of taking the matter further at that time apart from acquiring a small collection of photographs of the players depicted in the old magazine.

Following the suggestion of Christopher Martin-Jenkins, I approached Roger Mann, the West Country collector of cricket memorabilia, who might, he felt, be able to supply pictures of the early Hearne cricketers. It was Roger who so strongly urged that the research should be set down in book form, and it is not too much to say that without his continued encouragement this book might never have been written.

Appeals for information in family history journals and local newspapers resulted in correspondence with a grand-daughter of Walter Hearne, also a grand-daughter of Alec's sister who was able to locate Alec's grandson, Donald Marchant; all contributed family photographs and much factual information.

The local history sections of public libraries at Lewisham, Ealing, Canterbury, Rickmansworth, Stoke Poges, the Chalfonts and Missenden contained a lot of interesting material, the staff in all cases proving very helpful.

It seemed quite likely that there were descendants of Frank Hearne still alive in South Africa. Frank had emigrated in 1889 and his son G.A.L. Hearne had been a first class cricketer. Mark Tapping, the well-known South African genealogist, Shelagh Pike of Claremont, Cape Town, and A.C. Parker, sports editor of the *Cape Argus*, did some research which produced quite unexpected results, and letters were soon flowing to and from Frank's grandsons and great-grandson, all of whom were veritable mines of information, supplying many photographs some of which had been taken in England well before the turn of the century.

Grandfather Hearne's nephew, Harry Hearne, also from South Africa, suggested that a distant cousin in Harpenden, Hertfordshire, (another Frank Hearne), might be interested in the family story. This contact served to add several branches to the family tree, besides producing a second photograph of a Hearne family eleven comprising a somewhat different set of players from the one already in my possession. Frank also outlined our relationship to Eric Sturgess, the post-war South African tennis star.

With all the foregoing material and sources of information at my disposal, it will be abundantly clear that any misgivings that I might have had about committing the family history to print were soon swept aside, and I hope that it will be enjoyed by those interested enough to read it all.

Finally, lest it should seem strange that one who grew up with a first class cricket background should appear to be lacking in detailed knowledge of the game, it must be pointed out that cricket figured to such an extent in my early years that it was hardly given a second thought. Frequent visits to the somewhat awesome Lord's cricket ground, mixing with the players of the time (I was forever in the professionals' quarters), and visits to our home by many of these famous personalities, were everyday occurrences and did not mean much to a youngster who was more at home in his grandfather's wheelwright workshop, wielding a spokeshave and paint brush instead of a bat and ball. To me, a ripple of applause at Lord's frankly meant no more than the ringing of my grandfather's hammer on his anvil; in fact, the latter sound probably had more significance, as the John Hearne tradition of wheelwrights certainly goes back in direct line of descent for almost three hundred years, long before the date at which we can pinpoint the first cricketer.

After some deliberation it was decided not to arrange the chapters in chronological order but to follow each father with an account of his sons' careers, thus keeping each family group together where applicable. With so many of the cricketing Hearnes sharing common Christian names, there is plenty of scope for confusion. To help avoid this, each cricketer has a chapter to himself and the chapter number is shown on the family tree.

I have not attempted to give an exhaustive account of each player's performance, but have drawn attention to some of their best efforts. Wherever possible, however, I have included details of the family background and something of the character and personal life of these cricketing Hearnes.

The name of Hearne and its variants is not uncommon, occurring frequently in that part of Buckinghamshire where the cricketers originated, roughly a large rectangle extending from Great and Little Missenden eastward to Chesham, south to Chalfont St. Giles and Chalfont St. Peter, west to Beaconsfield and High Wycombe then north to Hughenden. The name can be traced back at least as far as the thirteenth century.

According to authoritative sources, the name derives from the local word for "residence in a nook or corner of land", "in a bend" or "in a curving valley" as at Hern (Kent) or Hirn (Hertfordshire). In Ireland, Hearne is the Waterford anglicised version of the more common surname Hern, which originates from the Irish for "horse-lord" dating back into the mists of time.

The earliest mentions of the name that I have discovered to date are Henry en le Hurne from the *Rotuli Hundredorum*, the Hundred Rolls of Buckinghamshire (1279), and John atte Hurn, who was fined in 1304 at Kingsclere, Berkshire, for "a house etc. taken from the waste".

In 1415 Thomas Hearne, vicar of Hughenden, Buckinghamshire, resigned within a year for reasons as yet unknown. (Was he guilty of playing cricket on the Sabbath?)

Although the cricketer Hearnes came from humble beginnings, numerous others of the name have achieved fame in different spheres of life.

The eighteenth-century artist Thomas Hearne is worthy of mention in view of the artistic talent which occurs in several of the cricketers and their children, although further research is necessary if a link is to be established with the artist himself. Another Thomas Hearne was the famous Oxford diarist and antiquary of the early eighteenth century, who asserted that he had a connection with the village of Penn. This is probably correct as numerous Hearnes are mentioned in "The History of the Village of Penn" by Gilbert Jenkins from 1558 onwards. Finally there is the late Richard Hearne, the actor so well known for his much-loved character Mr. Pastry. Those readers with a romantic turn of mind might consider that the legendary figure of Herne the Hunter, immortalized by William Shakespeare in *The Merry Wives of Windsor*, would be worthy of inclusion.

The intriguing question of when the Hearnes first began to play cricket cannot, of course, be answered, although an examination of the family tree provides ample ground for speculation. It will be noted that the cricketers descend from three brothers. Joseph (born 1794), William (born 1797) and Thomas (born 1800) who were among the numerous children of John and Mary Hearne, married in 1783.

My grandfather assured me on several occasions that William was a keen player, whilst William's brothers Thomas and Joseph certainly played a great deal. It therefore seems reasonable to assume that their father John, born in 1754, instilled the love of the game in his sons and probably played himself. With their skills as wheelwrights and carpenters they could easily have fashioned bats and stumps for the village teams.

The cricketers earned the love and respect of all who knew them. Proof of their excellent characters is given time and again by contemporary writers and their fellow players; in fact, the only blot on the family honour which has come to light concerns one John Hearne who was alleged to have illegally felled a beech tree near Penn, way back in 1666. Unfortunately, history does not record whether or not he was found guilty.

It would seem that Peter Hearn, who played for Kent C.C.C. during the 1950's, is not related to the cricketers who appear in the following pages; however, genealogical research has so often come up with the unexpected that who knows what the future may reveal?

Chapter 1

Thomas Hearne – 'Old Tom'
(Middlesex 1859-75)

THOMAS, the eldest son of Thomas Hearne and Elizabeth, was born on the 4th September, 1826, at *The White Hart*, Chalfont St. Peter, and derived his love of cricket from his father. The Chalfont Cricket Club's meetings were often held at *The White Hart*, so a cricket background was part of his life from his earliest days. He was later known as 'Old Tom' to distinguish him from his own eldest son Thomas Arthur, but sometimes confusion still occurs especially when reference is made to 'Old Tom's' father.

He first played for the local side at the age of fourteen, and a year later he went to the village of Harefield in North West Middlesex to learn the trade of a tailor, and thus follow in the footsteps of his father. The 1841 census for Chalfont St. Peter shows that the family had vacated *The White Hart* and were then living in the Goldhill part of the village. Thomas senior was devoting his time to tailoring in order to support his two sons and four daughters.

The same census return includes the author's great-great-grandfather, William the Wheelwright, and his son John who eventually took over his father's business. Their workshops, at the rear of *The George*, were only a very short distance from *The White Hart*, and they lived opposite the latter premises. Thomas and his younger brother George were closely acquainted with their cousin John and my grandfather would often repeat his father's stories about them when they were young boys.

At the time of young Thomas, Harefield was a very small rural village, probably even smaller than Chalfont St. Peter. However, the presence of a public house called *The Cricketers* (or *Cricket Players*) may have made him feel at home. There would have been very few shops in Harefield in those days, as many of the householders were self-sufficient for vegetables and would also have kept a pig. Flour would have been obtained from local mills along the River Colne. Most of the menfolk were employed in agriculture or were general labourers. Many essential goods were made by the local community, and the few shops probably consisted of converted living rooms of some of the private houses.

The 1851 census for Harefield gives a population of 1520 of whom 42 persons were associated with shopkeeping in the broadest sense, and this included two tailors. One was a Hale who had one apprentice; by 1871 Henry Hale (tailor) employed 4 men, so perhaps Thomas learned his craft from an early Hale.

In 1844 Thomas senior, the tailor, and his family moved to Bell's Hill, Stoke Poges, Buckinghamshire, where young Tom seems to have played cricket for most of the local clubs, including Eton and Beaconsfield. For some reason he returned briefly to Harefield in 1848, when he commenced to bowl round arm. Until then he had bowled fast underhand.

Stoke Poges in those days was another very small community, south of Stoke Common which still preserves its rural character. There were several large houses with grand estates in the vicinity, and it seems quite likely that Tom's first wife, Charlotte Clilverd, was in service at one of them. The fact that she and Tom were married at the parish church of West Hackney on 9th July 1849, her father John Clilverd being a shoemaker, indicates that she was not a local girl.

Tom's occupation at the time of his marriage is shown as a tailor at Stoke Poges, Buckinghamshire, where the young couple took up residence adjoining *The Sefton Arms*, and where their two sons were born. Tom's father was still in the tailoring business, living a short distance away at Bell's Hill with his wife and their two youngest daughters, Susannah, a "pupil teacher" aged 16, and Hannah, 14, who was still a scholar.

By 1849 Thomas's reputation as a successful cricketer was so well known among the local clubs that it came to the notice of Harvey Winson Fellows, a member of MCC. Impressed by the reports he received, Fellows rode over to Stoke Poges from his home in Rickmansworth and enquired at *The Sefton Arms* as to where he could find Tom Hearne the cricketer. He did not have to look far as Tom was standing outside his home at the adjoining cottage, and probably regretting the lack of a game of cricket on such a fine day. He immediately accepted Fellows' invitation to play for his team at Rickmansworth the same day. Upon being asked how he would get there, as it was some eight or nine miles from village to village, Tom replied that he would walk, apparently to the astonishment of Fellows.

However, walk he did; he took several wickets, made a lot of runs and then walked home after the match, turning over the events of the day in his mind. It proved to be a fateful game, for had he but known it, that day was to prove the first step on a path leading to a long and eventful career in the cricket world, due in no small measure to Harvey Fellows.

G.G. – J. – H. – W. – W. – G.F.
G.Sen – T.Sen – T.Jun   *c. 1880*
F. – R. – A.

Two Early Hearne XI's

Walter – H. – J.T. – William – J.
G.G. – G.F.   *c. 1895*
Billy – R. – T. – Alec

Harvey Winson Fellows, to whom Tom was so greatly indebted, was born at Rickmansworth, Hertfordshire, and initially lived in the family residence at Moneyhill House before moving to Riverside on the southern side of Uxbridge Road just on the western outskirts of Rickmansworth, where the back garden was bounded by the River Colne.

Whilst living there he formed his own cricket club, Riverside, on the land opposite to his house. I am indebted to Wilf Broughton of Rickmansworth for the following account:

"After his father's death Harvey Fellows became the principal attorney of Rickmansworth as well as a partner in Salter's Brewery and its chain of inns. He was a cricketer of the highest class, having learned the game at Eton and Oxford. In the Harrow matches he was a dreaded fast bowler. His long stop once had two fingers broken in stopping a ball from Fellows which 'hummed like a top'. In the Eton *v* Harrow match of 1822 there were 38 byes and 15 wides off Fellows' bowling in the Harrow first innings and 28 byes and 4 wides in the second. In *Wisden* he held the record of giving away 30 runs in wides and byes in one over in an MCC match at Lord's. Nevertheless he played for the Gentlemen against the Players between 1847 and 1851, the most important event of the cricket season before the introduction of Test Matches with Australia".

In the field he sometimes appeared as wicket-keeper or cover point, agile in spite of his bulky fifteen stones. Fellows' best years were from 1847 to 1850 when he was chosen for all the great matches by MCC, I Zingari, or the Gentlemen of England against the Players. His bowling against the Players in the 1847 match was remarkably effective. Fuller Pilch, usually a fearless batsman, was seen to turn away from Fellows' deliveries, and William Lillywhite, albeit 55 years old, asked for leave of absence rather than face Fellows. The score book reads 'Lillywhite refused to go in – 0' without his wicket being credited to Fellows.

Lord Harris declared that Fellows was the fastest bowler ever, and wondered how he made the ball 'hum through the air'. He suspected that the seam had become somewhat lifted. W.G. Grace, in his book "Cricket", stated that Fellows was dangerous to bat against and also confirmed this ability to make the ball hum like a top. He recalled occasions when Fellows knocked all the stumps clean out of the ground, and when he hit a stump so hard that it fell into the hands of long stop 11 yards behind the wicket. Grace described Fellows' bowling as between underhand and round arm. In later years, when he tried to bowl over arm, his pace was greatly reduced. Nevertheless an alphabet poem celebrating cricketers of the 1850's includes Fellows and describes him as having "electric speed with due precision blent".

As a batsman, he is credited with a hit of 132 yards whilst playing for I Zingari v. Gentlemen of Worcestershire. He often served on the MCC Committee and was the Club's legal adviser. Fellows died in 1907 and was buried wearing his I Zingari tie.

Tom Hearne was actively associated with the Rickmansworth Club for 11 seasons, and he also played for Hertfordshire County Cricket Club during the years 1849-1852.

One of the earliest club scores which includes Thomas Hearne is shown in a match played on 26th July 1849 between Rickmansworth and Harrow Town at Rickmansworth, illustrated in the Rickmansworth Club Bicentennial Book and reproduced with their kind permission:

Rickmansworth

First Innings		Second Innings	
Hale : b Royston	0	Hale : run out	10
Elliot : c Woodbridge b Royston	4	Elliot : b Woodbridge	0
Bone : run out	1	Bone : b Royston	0
H.W. Fellows : b Woodbridge	0	H.W. Fellows : b Royston	0
Hearne : b Royston	0	Hearne : b Royston	44
Percival : st. Hughes b Royston	3	Percival : c Page b Royston	0
Keene : b Royston	0	Keene : b Woodbridge	0
Kennet : b Woodbridge	0	Kennet : c Mackenzie b Royston	1
Plaistowe : b Woodbridge	0	Plaistowe : not out	0
Ayres : not out	0	Ayres : b Woodbridge	0
Byes and Wides	1	Byes and Wides	12
	9		78

Rickmansworth 1st innings all singles.

Harrow Town

Second Innings	
Hon. R.Grimston : b Fellows	21
Gray : c Percival b Hall	17
Hughes : b Hale	5
Royston : b Fellows	17
Mackenzie : b Fellows	13
Page : c Percival b Hale	4
Woodbridge : c Plaistowe b Hale	5
Philpot : run out	1
Dixon : b Fellows	0
Sims : not out	0
Byes and Wides	19
	103

Harrow won by 59 runs, having scored 43 in their first innings.

Harvey Fellows soon became so impressed by Tom's ability as an all-round cricketer that he mentioned him in praiseworthy terms to John Walker and his brothers who played cricket at Southgate. Known as the Walkers of Southgate, the seven brothers were excellent cricketers, six of them playing for the Gentlemen against the Players.

It is difficult to see why they all became famous players. Certainly their father, Isaac Walker, did not play much, but one of his brothers, H. Walker, was a keen cricketer who played for the Gentlemen twice against the Players and coached his nephews when he visited the family home at Arnos Grove.

Besides being fine cricketers, the Walkers were very capable administrators and the establishment of the Middlesex County Cricket Club in 1864 was due mainly to the energy of John Walker, the eldest brother. He became the County Club's first Vice President, a post he retained until his death, and the first committee of 16 included two of his brothers, Russell Donnithorne Walker and Vyell Edward Walker.

The brothers worked hard to ensure the well-being of the Club through all the difficult years when they were seeking a suitable ground, until a permanent home was finally found at Lord's. The Walkers played a very large part in the early days of the Middlesex Club, and their performances over the years are remarkable. Nor did they lack in courage in an era when batting was based on forward play on the rough and bumpy pitches of the day – some of which were positively dangerous – with the bowlers dominating the game for many years.

The Walkers continued to be the mainstay of the Middlesex County Cricket Club for many years, captaining the team between 1864 and 1884, at which latter date A.J. Webbe took over. V.E. and R.D. Walker followed each other as Presidents between 1864 and 1922.

The Walkers, influenced by the praise of Harvey Fellows, and knowing his protégé's reputation, had little hesitation in inviting Tom Hearne to play for them at Southgate, which he did with considerable success. It meant that he was now playing cricket in the company of distinguished players, for John Walker put together strong sides who played against such opponents as the United England Eleven, Surrey and other top clubs.

By 1851, the year of the Great Exhibition at the Crystal Palace in Hyde Park, Thomas was still playing for various local cricket clubs, including Ealing Dean. The Club's centenary history booklet records that 'Old Tom' was a pioneer founder and it is illustrated by a photograph of the members in 1851. This is one of the earliest pictures of Tom, showing him in a characteristic pose leaning on his cricket bat.

Attracted by the advantages that the Ealing district offered, including its proximity to Lord's and to Southgate, business possibilities and the residential qualification to play for Middlesex, Tom secured premises on the southern side of the Uxbridge Road, West Ealing, opposite the *Coach and Horses* public house. Here, in 1853, he opened a retail shop in connection with his profession as a tailor, and his younger brother, George Hearne, also moved into the area at about the same time. The shop, which comprised a two-storey building with rear premises and living accommodation on the first floor, still exists, with even the small board above the first floor proudly reading 'MCC House' in faded letters.

T. HEARNE,

TAILOR AND DRAPER,

UXBRIDGE ROAD, EALING.

CRICKET Bats, Balls, Pads, and Wickets. Flannel Shirts and Clothing of every description, suitable for the Game, on most reasonable terms. Gentlemen waited on at their own residences. A liberal allowance made to Schools. None but THE BEST articles supplied which T. H., being engaged at Lord's, selects himself.

Middlesex County Times, 14 March 1863.

Before the period when Tom Hearne moved to Ealing, the community was still largely rural in character, and in fact, at the beginning of the nineteenth century, Ealing was a picturesque part of the country with fewer than 3,000 inhabitants. Between the modest village and the metropolis to the east stretched several miles of countryside with no railways to serve it, and main communications were afforded by stagecoaches. By 1832 the population had more than doubled between the Acton boundary and the *Old Hatte Inn*, where there was large stabling for the West of England mailcoaches to change horses. The scene was rural, with a few groups of houses here and there, large areas of fields around several farms with market gardens, and an odd inn or two together with workers' cottages. One important centre of activity at that time was the *Green Man Inn* with stabling for a large number of horses.

In spite of his numerous cricket engagements, Thomas was first and foremost reliant on his skill as a tailor to earn a living. It was not uncommon for the more prudent of the professional cricketers to have a secondary occupation in case their playing careers were abruptly terminated by loss of form or injury. Whilst he was living at Ealing, Tom's census returns for 1861, 1871 and 1881 refer to his occupation as 'tailor and cricketer', 'tailor', and 'tailor and cricketer'.

The two brothers, Tom and George, were undoubtedly astute businessmen, and in 1855 they seized upon the opportunity to develop a piece of land situated at the rear of *The Green Man*, Uxbridge Road, West Ealing, as a cricket ground. A balcony at the back of the inn overlooked the rather small ground which had a cycle track around the boundary, all enclosed by a timber fence, which afforded little protection to the windows of the adjacent houses and those of *The Green Man* itself. Ealing Dean Cricket Club played there for many years up to 1912, when the site was sold for building, and apparently the Club Treasurer had to keep a careful record of the number of broken windows as, by standing agreement, the cost of replacement was half-a-crown for each broken pane.

One of the local club's annual matches at the end of the season was against a Hearne family eleven, well studded in the 1890's by several of their famous professional brethren.

Thomas was still playing successfully for Southgate during the mid-1850's, both he and his brother George appearing for them in 1857, and if Harvey Fellows can be said to have paved the way for his future, then John Walker certainly opened the door for him. In 1857, on Walker's recommendation, he was selected to play for MCC versus Sussex at Lord's on 15 and 16 June. He was then 30 years old, and although he may have appeared there earlier in one or two minor matches, this was his first game of note on the famous cricket ground with which he was destined to have close associations for the remainder of his life.

Thomas impressed his colleagues so well that he was subsequently chosen to play in the Grand Match between the All England XI and the United England XI at Lord's. The existence of two representative professional cricket teams stemmed from the resentment shown by some fourteen cricketers against the treatment and pay meted out by William Clarke, who had founded the All England Eleven in 1846. He had realized the enormous potential of being able to organise famous cricketers to play matches countrywide; hitherto there had been long periods when the professional players had no opportunity to employ their skills. Clarke changed all this and for six years he virtually dominated their playing lives, employing them on his own terms and making a great deal of money. Eventually some of the leading participants could put up with this state of affairs no longer and under the leadership of John Wisden the United England Eleven came into being. Much to Clarke's anger, Wisden's teams became as famous as his and Clarke refused even to consider a match between the two sides.

When William Clarke died in 1856 this absurd situation was changed under the leadership of George Parr who succeeded him, but apparently there was still a great deal of animosity and each team eagerly sought potential talent to the benefit of men such as Thomas Hearne.

In this Two Elevens' match he batted number ten in his side's first innings, making just a single run, thus his captain saw no reason to change the order and Wisden had him down to bat number ten again. However, the team was set 100 to win and upon being persuaded by John Walker, who knew Tom's potential more than Wisden, the latter allowed him to open the second innings, and not for the first or last time in his career Thomas fulfilled the trust put in him, for he scored 54 not out, and the United won by four wickets.

Two Elevens' Match

Lord's, 7 & 8 June 1858

United England Eleven won by four wickets

All England Eleven

J. Caesar	c Lockyer b Caffyn	0	c Hearne b Caffyn	0
A. Diver	b Caffyn	41	hit wkt b Grundy	17
H. Stephenson	c Ellis b Wisden	2	b Caffyn	21
G. Parr	run out	17	b Grundy	52
R. Tinley	c Griffith b Caffyn	12	b Wisden	10
G. Anderson	b Caffyn	0	b Caffyn	0
A. Clarke	b Caffyn	9	b Grundy	8
C. Brampton	b Caffyn	0	c Wisden b Caffyn	8
E. Willsher	b Wisden	0	b Grundy	6
J. Jackson	c Bell b Caffyn	10	not out	8
J. Bickley	not out	6	b Caffyn	0
Extras		14		13
		111		143

United England Eleven

J. Dean	b Willsher	6		
J. Grundy	b Jackson	0	not out	5
R. Carpenter	b Jackson	45	st Tinley b Parr	1
J. Lillywhite	b Jackson	1	b Jackson	7
W. Caffyn	b Jackson	26	c Finlay b Jackson	4
J. Wisden	c Willsher b Brampton	18	run out	2
T. Lockyer	b Jackson	16	b Stephenson	3
F. Bell	run out	1		
C. Ellis	not out	8	b Stephenson	15
T. Hearne	b Tinley	1	not out	54
G. Griffith	b Tinley	13		
Extras		20		9
		155	(for 6 wkts)	100

Tom did even better when the two sides met the following year, he and Carpenter scoring 149 for the first wicket. Carpenter made 98 and Tom 62 to celebrate the birth of his daughter, Lavinia Elizabeth Hearne.

In 1861 Thomas was in the Southgate team versus Eighteen of Enfield on 22nd and 23rd August when all seven of the Walker brothers played on the same side. The only other time the seven brothers all played for the local team was on 2nd and 3rd August 1860 when Sixteen of Southgate played the United All England XI, but on that occasion Tom was in the United side and proved to be the mainstay of the team's batting, scoring 32 and 42 out of totals of only 99 in each innings.

By this time Tom was acknowledged to be in the front rank as an all-round cricketer, and 1861 was a landmark in his career, for not only was he appointed to the ground staff at Lord's but he was also included in the pioneer English team which toured Australia under the captaincy of H.H. Stephenson.

In 1859 the first English cricket tour abroad had taken place when Parr's team visited North America, and it was so successful that the sponsors arranged a visit to Australia. The leading professional cricketers were approached, but several of them considered the financial terms were not sufficient, and refused the offer. Consequently, although the final side was a strong one, a number of the country's best players were not among the tourists, and Thomas Hearne may well have been lucky to be included as a replacement.

The team set sail from Liverpool on 20th October 1861 in Brunel's ship, the *Great Britain*, which had been converted after her North Atlantic run to cope with the route to Australia. The voyage around the Cape of Good Hope took over two months even in this grand ship, and the players were much relieved when they arrived at Melbourne to a magnificent reception from a huge crowd of over 10,000 folk.

The tour was a great success, large numbers of spectators attending the matches, whilst the team was royally entertained off the field to such a lavish extent that it is said they owed one of their very few defeats to the generosity of the refreshments.

In spite of a very tempting financial offer to remain in Australia for a further month, the team returned to England on 12th May. It must be said that apart from making 25 not out and taking two wickets against 21 of Tasmania at Hobart, and an innings of 37 not out in a drawn match at Ballarat, Tom did not do himself justice. Except for a few isolated instances the same can be said of other members of the Hearne family who took part in later overseas tours.

A Grand Cricket Match at the Cattle Market Ground, Islington
– an impression in watercolour by the author.

The first English team to tour Australia, 1861-62.
l to r: W.Mortlock, W.Mudie, G.Bennett, C.Lawrence, H.H.Stephenson, W.B.Hallam, W.Caffyn,
G.Griffith, T.Hearne, R.Iddison, T.Sewell Jun, E.Stephenson.

He was, however, still playing well for Southgate and scored 62 and 64 for them against Surrey Club and Ground at the Oval in 1862 when nobody else in the match made more than 30. This same year his brother George Hearne played his first match for the club. Tom's best innings that year was 134 for MCC & Ground *v* Sussex at Brighton.

1862 had seen the first London trams and although these were horse-drawn the pressure for public transport was beginning to bear results, for in 1863 the London Underground Railway was opened, running initially from Baker Street to Farringdon. Ealing was becoming a suburb of London and, in spite of the fact that the Great Western Railway Station at West Ealing was not built until 1871, Thomas Hearne's career and business were thriving. He had an advertisement in the 25th March 1863 edition of the Ealing Post, adjacent to one in the same column relating to the *Green Man Inn*.

In spite of Tom's success with both bat and ball – such as 54 for Southgate out of 126 against Oaidmures – it was not until 1863, when he was 37 years old, that he was first chosen for the Players versus the Gentlemen at the Oval. Opening the batting, he contributed a solid 36 which set the Players off to an impressive total of 353 and a subsequent win by 9 wickets.

On the 1st June of that year a 'Good Cricket Match' was played for Tom's benefit at Ealing, when the United South of England met Twenty-two of Ealing; unfortunately the weather was unkind and the event was said to have been . . . "no benefit at all".

In 1864 Tom and brother George played for Buckinghamshire against Middlesex on 2 and 3 June at Newport Pagnell when Tom made 2 and 28, George 7 and 11, and Tom took 7 wickets. Two days later they appeared for Middlesex versus Sussex at Islington; Tom scored 50, the club's first half-century, and produced the magnificent bowling figures of 9 for 63 and 5 for 48.

In August for the County against MCC and Ground, Tom opened the innings and scored 125, then took 4 for 49 and 3 for 42. This score of 125 made him the first Middlesex batsman to reach a century. He only just managed this record as T. Case, batting no. 5 in the same match, scored 116. George Hearne, no. 8 in the order, backed them up with a great 72. *Scores and Biographies* comments not only that Middlesex's 411 contrasted extra-ordinarily with their score of only 20 against the same bowlers – Grundy and Wootton – a few days earlier, but that only four of the twenty MCC wickets were bowled.

Middlesex *v* MCC & Ground

Islington, 1 & 2 August 1864

Middlesex won by an innings and 232 runs

Middlesex

T. Hearne	b Wootton	125
R.D. Walker	c Biddulph b Wootton	11
J. Frederick	b Wootton	9
E. Pooley	b Grundy	0
T. Case	b Grundy	116
I.D. Walker	run out	3
V.E. Walker	b Grundy	8
R.A. Fitzgerald	c Marsham b Grundy	0
G. Hearne	c & b Randolph	72
W. Catling	not out	24
D. Moffatt	c Randolph b Wootton	25
Extras		18
		411

MCC

E.G. Sutton	st Pooley b V.E. Walker	0	not out		13
S. Biddulph	run out	2	c G. Hearne b V.E. Walker		8
J. Grundy	c & b V.E. Walker	0	c Frederick b V.E. Walker		0
H.E. Bull	lbw b T. Hearne	32	b T. Hearne		12
C.B. Marsham	b V.E. Walker	6	hit wkt b V.E. Walker		13
T. Bignall	c Fitzgerald b T. Hearne	20	c I.D. Walker b T. Hearne		27
G. Wootton	c Case b V.E. Walker	10	st Pooley b V.E. Walker		0
L. Winslow	c & b V.E. Walker	0	b V.E. Walker		3
Capt. Trevor	c Fitzgerald b T. Hearne	8	c Catling b T. Hearne		4
G. Traill	not out	1	c & b V.E. Walker		4
J. Randolph	b T. Hearne	4	c Catling b V.E. Walker		0
Extras		1			2
		93			86

It is recorded that of the 241 runs made by T. Hearne and T. Case none were scored to leg.

In 1865 for Middlesex v. Hampshire at Islington on 1st and 2nd June, Tom failed to score, but bowled magnificently to take 5 for 50 and 5 for 35 as Hampshire followed on.

During these years there was no County Cricket Championship, but it was widely agreed that Middlesex had an outstanding team and indeed were acknowledged to be the best in 1866, which was also another successful season for Thomas when his fast medium bowling earned him 6 for 35 and 6 for 41 against Nottinghamshire; R.D. Walker's slow round arm deliveries accounted for the other eight victims. Thomas' best score was 146 against Surrey, again at Islington.

He was included in the Players team against the Gentlemen at Lord's that same year, 1866, a choice which caused much criticism – "croakers", as Ranjitsinhji described them. Tom once again rose to the occasion, and showed that although he was 40 years old, he was by no means a spent force, scoring 122 not out after being bowled by E.M. Grace in his first innings for 16. The Players won the match by 38 runs, their last victory until 1874. Tom's record for Middlesex in 1866 was outstanding. In 8 matches he averaged 35 with the bat and took 46 inexpensive wickets.

The Hearne brothers, Thomas and George, still played for Southgate in 1867, appearing together for the club on several occasions, and sometimes on opposite sides, as Tom was selected for the United South of England XI.

By now George Hearne was engaged by the Walkers to maintain the cricket ground at Southgate and coach the local team. Although Thomas saw his brother fairly frequently, their close and neighbourly association from then on was not so intimate, especially later when George moved to Catford. Thomas had suffered a tragic loss when his wife, Charlotte Ann, died on 28 April 1866. Charlotte had been a good and supportive wife, caring for the children and looking after the family business during the frequent and sometimes lengthy spells of her husband's absence. Perhaps not enough credit has been accorded to the women in this situation, many of necessity becoming better business folk than their husbands.

Thomas married again in 1867, this time to Caroline Ann Newton who had been born at Southall. The marriage took place on 30 December 1867 at Paddington Parish Church. Caroline's residence was in St. James, Paddington, where her father James Newton was a builder. On the wedding certificate, Tom's profession is characteristically shown as a "draper" rather than cricketer. They had one child, Kate Maud, born in 1871. Annie Hearne, as she was best known, first came to Ealing when she was sixteen months old, living to be the district's oldest inhabitant at the age of 96. The majority of those years were spent at MCC House where she managed the shop until shortly before her death in June 1927.

She recalled that in her childhood the fields of Ealing were famous for their violets, stretching to Perivale, and bright with daisies and cowslips. The Brent was then a cheerful rippling stream with banks full of bluebells. The old lady delighted to recount bygone days in her little back living room, the Sunday School treats on Ealing Common, the old-time fair on Ealing Green, coaches bringing life to the village before the advent of the railway, the great events at Manor House and other distinguished residences.

Annie was a woman of immense character and a worthy partner to Thomas; in her last few years one of her greatest pleasures was to entertain the younger generations of the family, and the author clearly remembers her near the end of her long life, sitting up in bed with a black lace shawl around her shoulders and a white lace cap on her head, like someone out of a Dickens novel, proffering softened chocolates from the top of a warm stove to her beloved small relatives.

In 1872 Tom was appointed superintendent of the ground bowlers at Lord's in succession to James Grundy, a task for which he was well qualified, as, apart from his own prowess with the ball, he was respected by his juniors and woe betide any of them who did not pull their weight. The 1872 season also saw Tom Hearne taking part in what was, for him, an unusual match at Lord's on 10 July, when he was actually included in the team of twenty-two men from the Lords and Commons to play the famous I Zingari side (probably the nearest he ever got to real politics). At that time he was still a force to be reckoned with, even at the age of 46; in fact only a few years previously he had made 122 not out for the Players versus the Gentlemen at Lord's. Whether this was uppermost in the minds of the I Zingari is not known, but before consenting to his inclusion in their opponents' team they stipulated that Tom should not bat, but would be allowed to bowl. This turned out to be a singularly disastrous arrangement, for he took 6 for 36 out of the I Zingari total of 72. It would have been better for them if he had only batted!

In 1873 the counties finally reached agreement on the vexed question of qualification, when it was decided that a player must make up his mind whether he should play for the county of his birth or for the county in which he lived. Although the County Cricket Championship was still only an informal arrangement and not fully accepted by the counties until 1890, it was nevertheless described as such by contemporary writers. Thomas Hearne was

T. Hearne
A lithograph by John Corbet Anderson
(Published 1859)

MCC House in 1926.

One of Tom's victims in 1866.

Tom in old age.

still appearing for Middlesex in 1874 and in 1875, but his active cricketing days as a professional were drawing to a close. During 1874 he did some umpiring, including the match between Middlesex and Nottinghamshire on 13, 14 and 15 July at Princes Ground, Hans Place, Chelsea. This was one of several cricket grounds with which Middlesex were associated before they finally settled on the present Lord's ground.

In 1876 MCC granted the Whit Monday match between the North and South at Lord's for Tom's benefit in recognition of his loyal services to the game over many years. Although the weather was not good, he received a satisfactory financial reward. That same year Tom played his last cricket match for Ealing, and virtually the last one of his life, although he and his brother George did turn out for the Hearne Family XI as late as 1886. Near the end of the 1876 season Tom suffered a devastating blow when a severe stroke of paralysis terminated his career as an active cricketer. It was feared in some quarters that he would never recover, but they did not know 'Old Tom', for the strong and determined man made such a fight against his disability that he recovered well enough to continue his work at Lord's for over twenty years more, and he became Secretary and Treasurer of the Cricketers' Fund Friendly Society after the death of John Wisden in 1884.

The year 1883 brought one more highlight in Tom's eventful life, for on 28 September his eldest daughter, Lavinia Elizabeth, who had been born at Ealing in 1859, married Frederick Raymond Wakefield, also aged 24, a jeweller from Cheltenham. The ceremony took place at the Parish Church of St. John, Ealing. Lavinia and her husband died in the influenza epidemic, which raged at the end of World War I, leaving their daughter Dorothy to be brought up at Thomas's home. Years later she married Edwin Sabin, who was then managing the sports shop for his cousin, John William Hearne.

Tom was the first professional to play for Middlesex before the formation of the present Club, and, in all the matches that he played for Middlesex between 1859 and 1875, he scored 1799 runs, average 19.77, and took 200 wickets at about 14 runs apiece. He averaged 35 with the bat and 13 with the ball during the two years following the formation of the Middlesex County Cricket Club.

There is one story which reflects the rapport between a shrewd and successful leader and a thoroughly professional cricketer who could be relied upon to do exactly what was expected of him by his captain, V.E. Walker, in a moment of high drama. In the Surrey v Middlesex match at Kennington Oval in 1868 the scores were level on the second day when the last man came in for Surrey. He was a young man named Roberts, playing in his first match for

Surrey, and expected to face the deliveries of Edward Rutter, a slow left arm bowler who had already taken 6 Surrey wickets. Walker, however, considered that the understandably nervous young man, with little experience, would be even more ill at ease if faced with the faster bowling of Hearne, so somewhat to everyone's surprise Tom was put on. Tom remained cool as ever, in spite of the tremendous excitement which died down to silence as he ran up to bowl and exploded into a mighty roar as he shattered poor Roberts' wicket with the first ball. The result was a tie.

Tom was a strong, well-built man, nearly 5 feet 11 inches tall, upright until very late in life, a man not to be easily ignored. This fact was remarked upon by an interviewer who reported in *Cricket. A Weekly Record of the Game* for 16 May, 1895 as follows: "Mr. Hearne's is a striking personality, upright when nearly approaching the traditional limit of life as half a century since, as keen apparently to take every halfpenny's change out of life as the youngest among us".

Apparently, Old Tom was initially somewhat irritated at being interrupted whilst engaged in bowling at the nets, as "a verb in the imperative mood was employed with reference to the unlucky interviewer". However, the old man soon relented enough to say: "I don't want to be advertised, for I've been here a long time, and I hope in the little time that's left to me that I shan't want another place. There's lots of people that have advertised me and put me in papers and photographed me and whatnot, but I keep going on in the same old way, and though I'm friendly with everyone, I don't care a (well, you may supply the blank) for any one".

"But lots of people will care to know about you?"

"Not they. I'm an old man now, and my work is most done. If I were a young fellow now like my nephew I'd be only too glad to talk to you and to be advertised".

It was suggested that he must have plenty of memories connected with cricket, which elicited the following reply:

"To tell you the truth, when I come to think about by-gone times, my old brains get so mixed and muddled that I can't clearly call 'em to mind at all. But Thoms – you know old Bob Thoms, well, he writes about cricket, and has put lots of things about me down in books and stories of the old days. You know, I never was much of a cricketer, not to say a player, but I've seen lots of curious things in my time . . . "

Soon afterwards a young man in a bright blazer came along, and Tom hailed his approach with evident relief:

"I'm afraid you'll have to let me go. There's a young prince . . . I'm afraid I'll have to go and wait on him. I'm not much of a man for newspapers and whatever you do, don't advertise me".

The reporter said that with these parting words the chief of the ground staff at Lord's hurried off, no doubt wishing his interviewer a speedy quittance. (Tom's mental farewell would have been in much more forthright and colourful terms!). Glancing back the younger man saw the old cricketer's now beaming face, with its circle of grizzled hair, welcoming his princely pupil.

The foregoing details accord very accurately with stories of Thomas the man and of his character which have been handed down by several generations of his family. If only he had known the interest shown in him by posterity, he would undoubtedly have been very surprised and, if truth is known, not a little pleased.

Thomas Hearne lived a long and, by any standards, successful life, during which he saw cricket emerge from the age of frequent squabbles and arguments between the various separate organisers to become the national game administered by MCC at Lord's.

There is no doubt that Tom was a much loved and respected man and his services were appreciated not only by the Middlesex County Cricket Club and MCC but also by club sides, as evinced by the Ealing Benefit Match in 1863 when the Stoke Cricket Club presented him with a bat and a purse for scoring 108 runs against a London club. Also, in November 1859, he received a handsome silver watch from members of the Ealing Dean Cricket Club as an acknowledgement of his six seasons with them.

He has been described as "essentially a man to send in early to take the edge off the bowling. Like all his family he was cool and collected and it is hardly likely that any bowler ever succeeded in frightening him out". (Interestingly enough this description could well describe another Hearne – J.W. or 'young Jack' as he was known, who played for Middlesex many years later).

Probably the best tribute to him was written by his friend the well-known umpire Robert Thoms in the issue of *Cricket. A Weekly Record of the Game*, for the 2 May 1889:

"Tom Hearne, of Middlesex and Lord's Ground, and one of my oldest associates on the cricket field, is an example of how an extra good man, who has shown form in what is termed outside cricket, may, if he gets the chance, soon prove that he can hold his own in first-class company. And that chance eventually came, but not until he had arrived at the mature age of thirty, having as I well know – and have oft seen – shown his prowess from sixteen years of age; for it may be truly said that there is hardly a green, common, heath, or cricket ground in the Home Counties on which he had not performed. In those days county contests had not been introduced to excite the population to which they now give rise, or it is very certain that Tom Hearne would not have been a roaming cricketer for all those years. As he was born in a county (Buckinghamshire) that did not aspire to greatness, and had no gate matches – for without this sterling feature, the gate, no county can or ever will succeed – it can well be imagined, in those times, the tempting offers that would have come in to either make a short cut to the Oval, or the equally lucrative county of the far north, Lancashire. But Tom was spotted after all by that most genial, kind-hearted, and liberal supporter of the game, the late Mr. John Walker of Southgate – would that we could recall him and the memorable Southgate days. To that gentleman he owed the 'push-off' which enabled him to get into the headquarters of cricket at Lord's, where he at once made his mark in the foremost rank and held it all through his active career, for no man has done more yeoman service for the MCC than Tom Hearne. Although some years ago, in the articles entitled "Cricket Sides and Notabilities" which appeared in the *Sporting Life*, under the head of Middlesex, I wrote the cricket character of Tom, I again take this opportunity of repeating that he was one of the very best all-round cricketers that ever batted for Middlesex or any other county, and that with the exception of "the Doctor, the Demon, or the Big-'un" (W.G. Grace), it would be difficult to name a cricketer who has surpassed him for consistency during the whole of his career. Although I had the pleasure of watching him in my official capacity from his start to finish in county contests, it would take me a long while to enumerate his doings; but writing as I now do from memory, I can recount that I have seen him on four different occasions top the century in great matches, and will now bring this sketch to a close by summing up the kind of cricketer he was. Tom was never a stylish or drawing-room batsman, but like unto the 'Little Doctor' (E.M. Grace) had a style of his own that could never be copied. He belonged to the order of batsmen who hit hard and often, spank the leather to the boundaries, upset the scores, and win matches; the useful but not showy sort, and of whom it may be said Mr. W.W. Read is now a similar example. Even in the days of rough grounds Tom would always have a good look and a go at the very fastest bowlers. I recollect how in his first great match at Lord's, when playing for the United *v* All England, in the second innings – when the match looked a gone coon – he laid on to Jackson and Stephenson and won the game for the United with a sparkling fifty-four not out. That he was a naturally gifted cricketer is proved by his turning from a fast underhand bowler into a rare good round arm trundler, which he acquired by practice bowling at Lord's. As a fieldsman, he could go all over the shop, and was a tradesman in all the departments; for he could keep wicket, long stop to the very fastest bowlers (Mr. Fellows), take point, or go into the country as long field; and that he could throw straight was proved during the match of Middlesex *v* Nottinghamshire at Islington in 1866, which feat I will relate. Tom was on at my end, and just about to deliver the ball to George Parr – the celebrated batsman – when a pigeon, out for a morning constitutional, came flying across the wicket, about 15 yards high. Without hesitation, Tom let go the leather, and with a fine straight shot brought down the bird, which he now retains in a preserved state as an heirloom to the family. Years have rolled by since he and I first met, and my best wishes will be that Old Tom, or 'Geneva' as I familiarly call him, may for untold seasons still be found in health and happiness on the green sward to which he has been so devotedly attached.

A few notes on chief incidents in Tom Hearne's career will serve as a suitable addition to Thoms' personal reminiscences of the veteran. It is not unfitting, we hope, that the opening day of the season at Lord's should have been chosen by *Cricket* to commemorate the long services of a Cricketer who, by his long connection with the Marylebone Club, as well as by virtue of his office as Treasurer of the Cricketer's Club Friendly Society, can claim to have done – in his way – not a little to promote the game . . . "

The notes then go on briefly to describe Tom's life and career up to the date of the article.

Thomas Hearne retired in 1898, the year Gladstone died, after 40 years service, on a pension of £30 per annum. His position as head bowler on the MCC staff was taken by G. Hay of Derbyshire. In the spring of 1900 Tom was taken seriously ill and for ten days he lay in a semi-conscious state, receiving little or no nourishment the whole time until at last even his great strength gave out. He died of apoplexy on the 13 May at his Ealing home and was buried at St. George's Cemetery, Hanwell. Among his family and the large number of cricketing friends and colleagues who attended the funeral there were many famous names.

Chapter 2

Thomas Arthur Hearne
(Groundsman – Lord's Cricket Ground)

BORN on 29 December 1849 at Stoke Poges, Buckinghamshire, where his father was then practising his trade as a tailor (in between playing as much cricket as he could), Thomas Arthur Hearne was the eldest child of 'old' Thomas. He also became a fairly good player but was never proficient enough to attempt to earn a living at the game. Instead, he developed a keen appreciation of cricket, especially the care and maintenance of the playing pitches and grounds.

As a young lad he made his first and never-to-be-forgotten appearance at the Oval on 10th September 1866, when he played for the Middlesex Colts *v* Surrey Colts. He made a 'duck' in each innings but did take two wickets for 13 runs. Five years later, on the 8th, 9th and 10th of May 1871, he had his first match at Lord's, when he was in the side of 15 Colts of England with Rev. O. Shore as Captain against MCC, which was another disappointing occasion for him as he was dismissed for another duck – caught and bowled Grace, second innings bowled Brune for 6. He was shown on the score sheet as 'T. Hearne jnr (Middlesex)'. At that time he was working as a tailor at Ealing, but found time to act as second ground bowler for the Ealing Cricket Club, where his father had such close associations.

On 7th August 1881, when he was 32 years old, Thomas married Mary Ann Day, aged 23, at the Parish Church of St. John, Ealing. Mary Ann, a spinster, was the daughter of Henry Day, a local gardener. The marriage certificate indicates that like Thomas she was also a tailor, so the couple almost certainly had more than romantic associations before they married. The witnesses at the ceremony were G.F. Hearne, Eliza his wife and G.G. Hearne.

Thomas Arthur became groundsman at Wellington College, Sandhurst, where he was employed until 1898 when he took over as Head Groundsman at Lord's. He soon became very popular with everybody especially the young members of his ground staff who soon learned that there was a heart of gold beneath the sometimes stern appearance. He was head of ground staff at Lord's when Patsy Hendren was a lad ostensibly selling score cards, which job he and other young colleagues often dodged to watch the cricket. The old man knew this went on but he was a person who understood the boys and their ways, and consequently discipline on these occasions was not too strict. While it may be true that Thomas Arthur resembled his father closely, as quoted in several quarters, by nature he inherited much of uncle George's humourous personality and when 'off duty' was always ready for a joke or playful prank, whereas his father was inclined to take a rather more serious view of life. He died at St. Bartholomew's Hospital on 29th January 1910, aged 61, of heart failure whilst being treated for a malignant growth, and was buried at Kingston Cemetery on 3rd February 1910.

Thomas Arthur Hearne resided at The Lodge adjacent to the old main entrance gate in St. John's Wood Road. The ground floor of the now enlarged building forms a shop with living accommodation on the first floor which is usually occupied by a member of the cricket staff. The 'Occupation' section of his death certificate states: "Groundsman at Lord's Cricket Ground, The Lodge, Lord's Cricket Ground, St. John's Wood".

The Annual Report of MCC for 1898 contains this reference to Thomas Arthur:

"Thomas A. Hearne, for many years Groundman at Wellington College, has been appointed Head Groundman in the place of P. Pearce. Tom Hearne (Thomas Arthur's father) has to the great regret of the Committee, after forty years' service, been compelled through ill health to resign his post of Head Bowler, which he had held for 26 years; a pension of £30 a year has been granted to him in recognition of his long and faithful services to the Club. George Hay has been appointed Head Bowler in Tom Hearne's place".

The following items in the MCC minutes also relate:

December 11th 1899
"The Finance Sub-Committee reported . . . an increase of salary to T. Hearne at 40/- a week".

No further mention of T.A. Hearne is made until:

December 13th 1909
"Authority was given to the Secretary to pay full wages to Tom Hearne during his absence in the hospital".

January 19th 1910
"It was decided to give a donation of £10 to St. Bartholomew's Hospital in consideration of the treatment received there by Tom Hearne".

February 7th 1910

"The Secretary reported the death of Tom Hearne, Head Superintendent of the ground".

"The Secretary reported that he had paid Tom Hearne's wages up to date and had sent a wreath to his funeral. He was instructed to discontinue the payment of wages and to find out and report as to the future intentions of Mrs. Hearne, the widow".

April 4th 1910

"A donation of £150 was granted to Mrs. T. Hearne. Instructions were given to the Secretary to dispense sums to this amount as required".

Annual Report, 1910

"By the death of Mr. Tom Hearne the Club has lost a servant who has conscientiously discharged the duties of Superintendent of the ground for 12 years. H.E. White of Hertfordshire has been appointed in his place".

Annual General Meeting, 1910

"The President . . . made a sympathetic reference to the losses sustained by the Club in the death of Tom Hearne the much respected groundman".

Thomas Arthur Hearne, looking not unlike King Edward VII, appears on the photograph standing between a steam traction engine and a massive heavy iron roller which it is pulling. The roller was aptly nicknamed 'Thomas Lord' and performed its important task for many years, hauled along by a beloved old horse and then by a number of lads on the ground staff. After World War II, 'Thomas Lord' was all but forgotten; however, he has now been renovated and occupies a dignified place in the Coronation Garden. An account of 'Thomas Lord's' loyal service is recounted in detail by Alan Hewitt in *The Cricketer* for September 1990.

Thomas Arthur as a groundsman.

Above and below right: George Francis Hearne

Chapter 3

George Francis Hearne
(MCC-1882. Pavilion Clerk – Lord's Cricket Ground)

GEORGE FRANCIS HEARNE, son of 'Old' Thomas Hearne and younger brother of Thomas Arthur, was also born at Stoke Poges, his birthday being the 18th October 1851, and like young Tom he spent much of his early life at Ealing. He was a very good all-round cricketer and an excellent long-stop. Contemporary records indicate that had he adopted cricket as a profession he might have done very well because even with the limited amount of cricket he did take part in he showed himself to be a very good player. At present there is no record of his activities until 1872 when he became Pavilion Clerk at Lords (this is according to *Cricket. A Weekly Record of the Game* of the 9th May 1907 whereas a later issue of this same periodical dated January 28th 1909 states he commenced duties at Lords in 1873).

As a result of obtaining permanent employment he felt secure enough to support a wife and on 22nd November 1874 he married Eliza Bridgeman at the Parish Church of St. Peter, Stepney. Both were 23 years old and Eliza's late father had been a porter. George Francis's occupation is shown as a 'Merchant's Clerk' on the marriage certificate. They lived at 3 Sunnyside Road, Ealing and eventually had three daughters and four sons, one of whom, Thomas John Hearne, claims recognition in first class cricket records in a very unusual way, as will be seen later.

Lord's was a very different headquarters of cricket from that which most readers will remember and know, and as different again from the ground on which his father, 'Old Tom' Hearne, played his first match in 1857 when Lord's was distinctly rural with stables for the visitors' and members' horses. The pavilion looked like a provincial clubhouse set in a field with, to say the least, a very rough pitch; the first regular groundsman was not employed until 1864 and work did not commence on the present pavilion until 1889.

In the early days hockey, lacrosse and baseball matches were played there. Other activities included pony races, archery and dancing and once even a

Red Indian encampment was constructed there. Second to cricket the other main pursuit was tennis, and today Lord's still boasts one of the few Real Tennis courts in the country.

Upon the purchase of the freehold of the ground in 1866 work commenced on the construction of the Grandstand. Before its completion there had been no facilities for the press and reporters had to sit or stand wherever they could. It was demolished in 1929-30 when the existing building was erected.

It is not within the compass of this book to trace the history of this famous cricket ground in detail. It will suffice to say that the cricketer Hearnes were closely associated with the important formative years of its development, all of which have been so well recounted and illustrated by well known cricket writers and players.

George Francis started work under J.A. Murdoch with whom he was associated for over 30 seasons. Murdoch had been appointed in 1872 as a successor to Sydney Dark who was Assistant Secretary to MCC and Clerk to the Committee. G.F. carried on his job at Lords for 36 years and was forced to retire in 1908 due to an accident when he fell heavily down a long circular staircase. He may have completely recovered from this first accident had he not had another fall six months later injuring his head on the same spot. As a result he resigned his post and was gratified to receive a pension from MCC in appreciation of his services. Although it has been stated that G.F. "was not an outstanding player" he nevertheless had the unusual record of playing cricket in MCC matches for no less than 32 consecutive seasons. Also, just as remarkably, he captained a side for 36 years without a break. Naturally he did not play in every match over this long period as his work sometimes prevented that. The Club concerned was originally known as the St. John's Wood Ramblers a name which was afterwards changed to the Cross Arrows.

This is a convenient point to touch briefly on the history of the Cross Arrows Cricket Club. A detailed account of the Club appears in an informative book written by Richard (Dick) Gaby in 1980 to commemorate the Club's centenary and he kindly consented to the following details about the founders of the Club being quoted from that story.

"Prior to 1880 the staff at Lord's played away matches against other local cricket clubs and it is believed that at that time they called themselves 'St. John's Wood Ramblers Cricket Club'. However, it was discovered, so the story goes, that in the locality there was another Club of the same name and it was therefore decided in 1880 that the Lord's Club should be re-named the "Cross Arrows Cricket Club".

It appears from the notes that have been handed down from various sources that among the founders of the Cross Arrows Cricket Club were the following people:-

J.A. Murdoch.................................Assistant Secretary, MCC
G.F. Hearne..................................Chief Clerk, MCC
G. Lambert...................................Tennis Marker
Ben Peggs ....Rackets Marker
J. Fennell ....Assistant Tennis Marker
P. Need ....Pavilion Dressing Room Attendant
W.H. Slatter..................................Painter
R. Gaby.......................................Lawn Tennis Professional

and, no doubt, there were others whose names are not recorded.

Soon after the Club had been founded, Rules were drawn up and Rule 2 stated "That the members shall consist of MCC employees only". A few years later the Rule was amended so that certain non-MCC employees could be admitted, and Ben Warsop the renowned cricket bat maker of that time, was one who was elected a member under this Rule. He took great interest in the Club and played for the Club on many occasions. (The current Rule is more specific and allows for the election of 'Full Members' consisting of MCC and Middlesex employees, past and present, male and female, and 'Associate Members' may be elected at the discretion of the Committee. Female members of the staff were first elected in 1953)".

It will be noted from the foregoing that G.F. Hearne and R. Gaby, the father of the author of the book *The Cross Arrows C.C.*, were among the Founder Members. R. Gaby Senr. remained a member of the Cross Arrows and, before he died in 1940, was the last surviving Founder.

George Francis also has another distinction – he became the first member of the Cross Arrows to score a century when he knocked up 127 runs in 1886. He had been taught to play cricket by his father 'Old Tom', on *The Green Man* ground at Ealing which his father and uncle George laid down in 1855.

When G.F. first went to work at Lords he was with the then Hon. Secretary to MCC, R.A. Fitzgerald, for three years. At that time there was not much clerical work to be done so he was directed to bowl at the nets and play in away matches when required. He also assisted Fitzgerald during bigger matches at Lords such as Oxford *v* Cambridge and Eton *v* Harrow. However, when the membership of the Club increased he had to spend less time playing cricket and devote more time to his office duties.

R.A. Fitzgerald was a very popular gentleman with the members and during his working period at Lord's, about the middle of the 1860's, the Club purchased the freehold of the ground. During the 13 years he was Secretary the membership increased from 650 to 2080. Fitzgerald's health was not good and he was forced to take a long sea trip in an effort to recuperate but on his return to England he was never able to resume work at Lord's and died a few years later. Whilst he was away his work was carried on by Henry Perkins who succeeded him in 1876.

George Francis Hearne as a young boy witnessed the death of the pigeon referred to in Chapter I and, excited by the event, ran onto the field and was given the dead bird which was subsequently stuffed and preserved as an heirloom by the family. It was on display during the Imperial Victorian Exhibition at the Crystal Palace in 1897, and is now in the possession of G.F.'s grandson David Hearne.

The showcase bears the following inscription:

Killed by T. Hearne
with a cricket ball
while playing the
Notts v. Middlesex cricket match
August 9th 1866.

G. Mills Bird & Animal Preserver.

Another famous Lord's figure of this period was James Henry Dark. G.F. recalled him in an interview he gave to the magazine *Cricket* for the 28th January 1909:

"I saw him several times, but he died before I went to Lord's in an official capacity. He was generally spoken of as 'The Boss' – the fact that he was at one time proprietor of Lord's is recorded on his tombstone – for the staff were engaged by him and he was a man who liked to have his own way in everything. He was given to speaking his mind freely, and once so angered my father by a remark that he left the ground in a huff and very likely would not have gone there again had not the Hon. Robert Grimston, hearing what took place, run after him and brought him back. The two were good friends afterwards, and when my father returned from Australia in 1862 he brought the old gentleman a gold nugget scarf-pin as a keepsake. Very many people seemed afraid of Dark, but he was alright when you knew him. He kept a white pony at the ground, I remember, and used to drive it about the neighbourhood harnessed to a chaise. He had a parrot too which possessed a somewhat remarkable vocabulary most of which is unprintable. For very many years he used to charge the Eton and Harrow boys 7s. 6d. each for playing at Lord's, which, considering the profit he made out of their match, was not considered quite 'the thing' and so the custom was discontinued after the season of 1862".

J.H. Dark was associated with Lord's for fifty-nine years and authorative sources have expressed the opinion that he probably did more for MCC than anyone else. He certainly deserves great credit for keeping things going during precarious periods of the ground's uneasy days when he seems to have used every facility available to satisfy his acute business mind.

G.F. further reminisces:

"My first out-match for MCC was in 1873 against Hastings, who had Mr. A.H. Stratford, several of the Phillips family and John Relf playing for them. The last-named was father of A.E. and R.R. Relf, who now play for Sussex, and was engaged at Wellington College with my brother Tom. He was a fair bat and a most accurate bowler. He delivered the ball with his hand only just above the shoulder, and never sent down a bad one. My father, who made 62, kept jumping in at the good length ones and driving them to the ring. When I was in with him he kept saying to me, "Why don't you hit like that?" But it took me all my time to play correctly, and I dared not attempt to take liberties. Going in at No. 8 I managed to carry my bat for 26 and in consequence was given a very nice notice by Kelly King, who was then the leading cricket reporter. The remarks coming from him were a great compliment, for he was not given to throwing bouquets. Once, when the St. John's Wood Ramblers were on tour, we met a very strong side at Brighton, including Mr. W. Newham, Stubberfield, Harry Killick, and the brothers Humphreys. The ground was very fast, and just as Alec Hearne was about to bowl to Mr. Newham, George Lohmann called out to me at point, "You're too close, you know. If he hits, you won't escape". I did not move, however, and the batsman got well hold of the ball, which I caught in my stomach, much to the wonder of those who were watching from the pavilion, which was directly behind me. As Mr. Newham went out he said to me, "You know about that, don't you?" It really was a wonderful catch, but I felt the blow for years afterwards. My highest innings at Lord's was 100 about thirty years ago – for Ealing and District v MCC, who had Mycroft and Clayton to bowl for them. Mr. J.S. Russell, the MCC captain, kept Mycroft on for a very long time, and as I always liked fast bowling I naturally appreciated it".

G.F.'s only first-class appearance was for MCC against Somerset in 1882 when he scored 26 in a total of 506 in a drawn game.

In the winter of 1884-5 George Francis Hearne together with Shaw and Shrewsbury went to Australia with Lillywhite's team although G.F. of course was not a member. He made the trip for the benefit of his health together with Henderson of Surrey who went for the same reason. Apparently they both enjoyed themselves very much and even persuaded the captain to let them play in a few up-country matches. G.F. was so attracted to Australia and felt so well when he was there that he would have liked to have gone again had the opportunity arisen.

It usually fell to George Francis to assemble the family Hearne XI which is not surprising in view of his occupation, a tidy mind and a capacity for organising, coupled with a caustic wit. The task was probably not very onerous as there was no lack of suitable players, ranging from grandfathers to young sons and nephews. The fact that they were prepared to travel considerable distances indicates a united spirit in the family, who undoubtedly looked on the occasion as an opportunity to exchange the latest gossip and meet relatives seldom otherwise seen.

G.F. recalled: "We played on *The Green Man* ground at Ealing, and the matches proved very attractive. The late William Hearn of Hertfordshire played for us in at least one of the games, but the match did not lose any of its interest in consequence, for, although he spelt his surname without the final 'e' he was related, though distantly, to us. Both branches of the family came from Buckinghamshire, and the different spelling is accounted for by the fact that William's grandmother, who was not very handy with her pen, thought it would save her a little trouble if she discarded the 'e'. The son and grandson were taught to do the same, but there is no doubt as to their connection with us. Tombstones and registers were searched and the relationship established".

On one occasion in 1884 the family eleven, and no doubt their supporters, travelled to Windsor in a horse brake and pair driven by William Gurney to play the Guards team. Needless to say the Hearnes were victorious and rejoiced at the fact that Joseph Hearne hit a delivery clean over the adjoining barracks.

A typical match score versus Ealing Dean Cricket Club, which appears to have been an annual event, is set out below and appeared in the *Middlesex County Times* for 24th September, 1887. In each case where the matches were reported there is an account of a dinner and a smoking concert in the evening during which Alec and George Gibbons could be relied on to sing.

Ealing Dean C.C. *v* Eleven Hearnes
Ealing, 24 September
Hearnes won by 10 runs

ELEVEN HEARNES		EALING DEAN	
F. Hearne, c sub b Pilling	24	G. Perkins, c A. Hearne b G.G. Hearne	40
G.F. Hearne, b Pilling	1	A. Farnden, st P. Hearne b Alec Hearne	1
W. Hearne, c Perkins b Sanders	9	J. Sanders, b A. Hearne	23
Alec Hearne, c and b Perkins	52	W. Barrett, c P. Hearne b H. Hearne	23
G.G. Hearne, b Shepherd	25	W. Williams, st P. Hearne b Alec Hearne	33
Walter Hearne, c Sanders b Perkins	20	W. Robinson, b Alec Hearne	10
A. Hearne, run out	8	S. Shepherd, not out	11
P. Hearne, run out	23	F. Sanders, b Alec Hearne	15
T. Hearne Snr., st Williams b Perkins	11	G. Pilling, b G. Hearne	8
J. Hearne, b Perkins	0	R. Swabey, b G. Hearne	3
Ben Hearne, not out	5	L. Swabey, c G.F. Hearne b Alec Hearne	3
Extras	16	Extras	14
	—		—
	194		184

On the 17th September 1894 G.F. was granted the great privilege of a benefit match at Lord's in recognition of the work he had carried out as Pavilion Clerk to MCC for twenty two years, the teams being the Gentlemen of the South *v* Players of the South. Many of the great players of the day turned out for him, including W.G. Grace, W.L. Murdoch, Sammy Woods and Bobby Abel.

"Pavilion Gossip" in the 1894 issue of *Cricket. A Weekly Record* quotes:

"On conclusion of the first day's play a gathering took place in the dining room of Mr. Reade's tavern where the beneficiary was the recipient of a little present from the boys of the Foundling Hospital. It has been a kindly act of Mr. Perkins, the MCC Secretary, to give admission this season to the Foundling School Eleven to five of the Club matches and, to show how they appreciated that privilege and Mr. G.F. Hearne's invitation to the 80 senior boys to witness play yesterday and today, they subscribed funds for the purchase of a handsome scarf pin for him, the head of which consists of three stumps with a bat across and a diamond representing a ball in the centre. The pin was enclosed in a case on which is a silver shield with the following inscription: "Given to G.F.H. by the Foundling Boys September 17th, 1894". The presentation was by Hine-Haycock and a complete surprise to G.F., who suitably returned thanks in the presence of Dr. W.G. Grace and his son, Mr. Ford, Mr. Bruce and Mr. Arthur Hay and numerous members of the cricketing staff at Lords, Robert Thoms the well known umpire, George, W., and J.T. Hearne, Mr. & Mrs. Hearne senior, and a large number of professionals as well as the headmaster, steward and cricketing staff of Foundling Hospital".

After the accident which caused his retirement G.F. returned to Ealing to reside in 1909. Shortly afterwards his wife Eliza died on 10th May 1910 and in 1914 he moved to Wellington Road, St. Albans, probably to be near one of his family, and he died at 16 Hedley Road on 30th May 1931, aged 79.

G.F. left four sons and two daughters; another daughter, who had married Fred Burton, the Hertfordshire cricketer, had died some years earlier. The mourners included his grand-daughter Miss D. Burton, his son F. Hearne and sons-in-law F. Burton and E. Tarver.

Chapter 4

Thomas John Hearne
(Middlesex 1908)

NUMEROUS cricket records have been achieved by the cricketing Hearnes over the years, but none so strange and unique as the one credited to Thomas John. It is also one not likely to be equalled, and is quoted in Wisden.

Thomas John Hearne was one of several children of George Francis Hearne, being born on 3rd July 1887 at 3 Sunnyside Road, Ealing. This street, off the western side of St. Mary's Road, is a very short distance south of Ealing Green in the vicinity of Walpole Park. It is still a very pleasant part of old Ealing, with some fine trees and large houses, retaining the character of years gone by.

Very little is known about Thomas John's early youth. He certainly developed into a promising cricketer when quite young and was actively connected with the game in one form or another for a livelihood, but knowing the family caution about not putting all one's eggs in one basket, he readily found additional sources of employment with his father's cousins George Gibbons and Alec constructing numerous cricket grounds during wintertime and coaching during the summer.

He commenced his professional career at the age of eighteen when he began playing for Berkshire; he was their stock slow left-arm bowler for three seasons until he joined the Middlesex CCC ground staff.

When he was 21 years old he was selected to play for Middlesex at Lord's against the Philadelphians, a touring side from America. Although they never attracted large crowds to watch their matches, the Philadelphians were nevertheless the major touring side in 1908 and could be a formidable team to beat. Ten years earlier, the Americans had been able to boast a team nearly as strong as England or Australia.

However, the invitation for Thomas John to play at Lord's arrived too late for him to get to the ground in time to bat. (A similar situation had been experienced by John Thomas Hearne eighteen years previously). History relates that Thomas John never actually set foot on the field at all during the match, which is rather strange as Middlesex won by seven wickets on such a treacherous wicket that the game was over in a day. Tarrant and Trott took all their opponents' wickets, bowling unchanged in both of the tourists' innings, 32 wickets falling in the day for 229 runs. But there seems no logical reason why T.J. did not field during the Americans' second innings, and there is no trace of an explanation.

That same year, 1908, Thomas John was included in the Middlesex second eleven against the Kent second eleven when he batted No. 11 and scored twelve runs. Apparently he did not bowl, although this was his strongest asset.

Tom served in the King's Royal Rifles during the 1914-1918 War, when tragically he was gassed in France and later had a foot crushed by a tank. As a result of these misfortunes he gave up all notions of becoming a first-class professional cricketer, and decided to concentrate on coaching and ground work for which he was now well qualified. He did not abandon his playing altogether, appearing a few times as a professional for Berkshire CCC in 1922 and 1923.

During this time, on April 8th 1922, Tom married Edith Fanny East at the Register Office, Wycombe, Buckinghamshire; the marriage certificate shows his occupation as a "professional cricketer". Edith's father, Robert William East, was a local gamekeeper; knowing the family fondness for shooting and fishing it seems quite likely that the couple became acquainted due to Tom and Robert having common interests.

The eldest of their two sons, David Bridgeman (named after his grandmother, wife of George Francis Hearne), was born on March 24th 1932 at the Maternity Home, Museum Road, St. Giles, Oxford. His parents' residence is given as Radley Park, Abingdon, Berkshire, for now Tom had secured employment at Radley College where each summer term he coached the cricket first XI. One of Tom's contemporaries who knew him well in 1925 says "He was an excellent coach. His slow and guileful bowling and his ability to bowl just the length required of each ball were tremendous assets to start with. In addition he had an understanding knowledge of the technique of batting, and knew how to modify that technique in the light of each individual boy's ability and potentiality. He was not a talkative coach, but to those who had ears to hear, his remarks, both critical and constructive, and his demonstrations of stroke play, were of enormous value." These characteristics sound very similar to the methods adopted in later years by John William (J.W.).

At about this time, Tom was giving serious consideration to obtaining a more permanent and full-time job. Fortunately, Bryanston School, Blandford Forum, in Dorset, had just become established in 1928 and he secured the

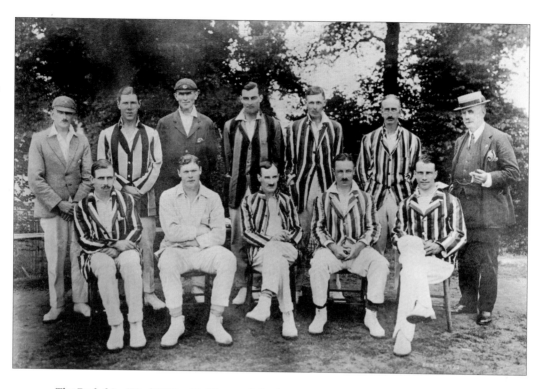

The Berkshire XI of 1923 with Thomas John first left in the back row and a forthcoming England captain, Percy Chapman second from the left in the front row.

Thomas John Hearne aged 19.

post of head groundsman/cricket coach and immediately set about the formidable task of creating playing-fields out of the river meadows. He first sought the opinion of his early "employer", George Gibbons, who, although over seventy years of age, made the long journey from Catford to Bryanston and gave valuable advice. Local opinion was that the task was well nigh impossible, but after watching the floods come and go for a few months during the winter of 1927-28 Tom said he could do it. With a small amount of local labour, he set to work removing the turf over all that area which is now the cricket field, levelling and draining, and replacing the turf to complete a magnificent piece of work. In the process several large beech trees had to be removed, root and branch. The results of this highly successful work are appreciated by all Bryanstonians, and those first-class rugger and hockey pitches, among the best in the country, lasting in such good condition to the end of each season, are a perpetual and fitting tribute to Tom Hearne's skill in their creation and care.

Unfortunately his health began to fail and through the war years it could have been only sheer will-power that many times kept him on his feet (he was umpiring a cricket match only ten days before he died) and keeping the grounds going under the difficult war-time conditions must have been an additional strain on his limited physical resources.

After Tom's death in 1947 a close friend paid him the following tribute:-

"I, for one, shall miss him in many ways: brief chats over the garden fence as he wheeled his bicycle up the beechwood path; chats generally about the garden or cricket reminiscences; meeting him outside the Common-room as he waited for his daily interview with the cricket master; watching him coaching in the nets, umpiring in a match – when Tom lifted his finger you knew you were out, all right – and many other daily episodes that, like so many of the good things of life, one just took for granted. Now they are only a memory, but a memory well worth having, of a very good friend and one who served the school so well and faithfully for twenty years".

Tom was succeeded as head groundsman by his eldest son David who had been working with his father since he left school. David retired in 1988 after 51 years' service and he, in turn, was followed for a short time by his third son Barrie. He in turn became head groundsman at Daniel Stewarts Melville College Edinburgh before securing a similar post at Radley College, where his father was employed so long ago, thus ensuring continuity of the groundsman/coaching tradition of the cricketing Hearnes.

Chapter 5

George Hearne - 'Old George'
(Middlesex 1861-68)

GEORGE, like brother Thomas, was born at *The White Hart*, Chalfont St. Peter, Buckinghamshire, on 15th May 1829. He did not receive any special training for a trade or profession in his younger days but he had a liking for horses. Various records confirm this; for instance, his wedding certificate describes him as a coachman, an Ealing Census return for 1861 shows him as an ostler, and on the birth certificate of his son, Alec, he is a horsekeeper. However, George was a man of many parts and was described as a grocer on the birth of his first son, George Gibbons Hearne, in 1856. Between times he worked on the preparation of cricket grounds and it is this latter occupation which eventually formed his main employment, supplemented by appearances as a professional cricketer.

His son Frank, then living in South Africa, wrote: "My father in 1860 had a livery stable, also several horses which he let out for ladies to ride; he also had two trotting horses. At the same time he was running a coal wharf; this was at Ealing in Middlesex".

George was quite a different personality from his elder brother, and whilst it may not be altogether true to say that he was happy-go-lucky, he did not regard life in general with the more serious attitude of Thomas. He had a great sense of humour and enjoyed a practical joke as evinced in contemporary writings and he never tired of recounting comical stories of incidents on the cricket field, laughing most of the time at his own yarns. In this respect his eldest daughter, Rose Mary, resembled him, a lady well remembered by her granddaughter, Beryl Winfield, as full of fun and laughter.

It is doubtful if George played quite as much cricket as his brother in his early years, but they were a very close-knit pair of men, especially when they were young. What Thomas said or did was usually right by George. *Cricket. A Weekly Record of the Game* states that he followed Thomas to Rickmansworth to work and play, but there is no evidence to support this. However it is certain that they both moved to Ealing around 1853, when Ealing was regarded as a northern section of the Brentford district, a situation which caused much concern to Ealing residents who understandably felt that they should manage their own affairs. Eventually in 1863 municipal functions for the parish came into being in the form of the Ealing Local Board.

George married Mary Gibbons, the daughter of a farmer from Rackenford, Devon, on 20th December 1854 at St. Mary's Church in the parish of St. Marylebone, when he was 25 years old and she was 26. Mary was in domestic service at the time as there was little prospect of other employment for a young woman in her small home village. They gave their address as 38 Queen Street and the ceremony was witnessed by James and Susannah Hearne. The newly-wedded couple came to reside at Hornton Cottages in what was Ealing Dean, now West Ealing, then a rural neighbourhood. Their home, adjacent to open fields, was situated on the southern side of the Uxbridge Road, a little west of the junction with Northfields Avenue opposite *The Green Man* where George and Thomas laid out a cricket ground; both the Cottages and *The Green Man* have since been demolished. George and Mary had four sons and two daughters, all born in Ealing, except for the youngest, Randolph.

In 1856 their first son, George Gibbons, was born; years later when father and son were both playing in the same match, a cricket reporter and compiler of Wisden named W.H. Knight wrote the younger man down on the score sheet as "George Hearne junior, son of Old George". The 'old' stuck; but the son was known variously as 'G.G.', 'young George' or 'wee Georgie' due to his small stature.

'Old George' Hearne was an active horse-dealer at Ealing for eleven years and probably chose to live where he did on account of the opportunities afforded by the close proximity of the busy coaching inns, *The Old Hatte* and *The Green Man*, and also the nearby open fields which could provide grazing for his horses. At that time the Uxbridge Road was a main coach route from London to the West of England and, in addition to passenger traffic, carried a heavy volume of farm vehicles to the old Covent Garden fruit and vegetable market.

Since his elder brother was well established with the Southgate Cricket Club, it will come as no surprise to the reader to learn that George was also engaged by the Walkers. There appears to be some confusion as to when he actually first played for them. In *The Walkers of Southgate* by W.A. Bettesworth one account includes him as a newcomer in 1856 along with the other well-known players of the time such as Henry Perkins, Charles Absolon, Coppinger and E. Willsher, whereas later it is stated that his first match was in 1862 against the Harlequins, who trounced Southgate. George scored 18 in the second innings but was 'absent' in the first! It has been said that George did not think he would be considered for selection and had not even bothered to check on the team sheet; doubtless the Walkers had more than a little to say to George on the matter.

By that time George had made his first appearance at Lord's on 16, 17 and 18 July 1860, aged 31, for the Colts or Pros. who have never played at Lord's *v* MCC. Unfortunately he failed to score in the first innings but fared a little better in the second innings, making 19 before being bowled by Jemmy Grundy.

George Hearne played cricket for both Buckinghamshire and Middlesex in the same seasons, as did his brother Thomas, but whilst Tom was frequently a member of the former county team it would appear that George only played for them on one occasion. During this time players could turn out for whichever counties they had connections with; the "County" games were really very informal and for most of the time the so called "qualification" rule was not treated seriously, but there were soon to be some rumblings from the press.

In 1864 the present Middlesex County Cricket Club was formed, although there had been "Middlesex" sides playing for many years before then. The newly-formed County Club played their first match at Newport Pagnell versus Buckinghamshire, who included George and Tom Hearne in their team.

The Middlesex side included B.B. Cooper who, after making a few appearances for Middlesex and for Kent, eventually settled in Australia and played for his adopted country in the inaugural Test Match at Melbourne in 1877. Also in the Middlesex side was Edward Pooley who would have played in that first Test Match had he not been unavoidably detained by the law in New Zealand over a gambling dispute. Surrey-born, Pooley made 256 appearances for his native county as against only 7 for Middlesex. He was considered the finest wicket-keeper of his day (when sober) but curiously Cooper seems to have kept in this match, at least in the second innings.

On 20th, 21st and 22nd June 1864, at Islington, George and Thomas Hearne appeared on opposite sides when the United All England Eleven beat Mr. C. Absolon's Twenty-Two. The United XI scored 331, Tom making 40 before being caught by brother George. The Twenty-Two totalled 163 and 122 with George making useful contributions in each innings.

This was the same year that Middlesex commenced playing at their first ground, the so-called Cattle Market Ground at Islington (see illustration on page 22) situated between the cattle market and the railway line. Thomas Case, the then Middlesex opening batsman, has described it as 'somewhat unprepossessing' and one can well imagine why.

The entrance was near to *The White Horse* at the junction of Market Road and Pedlar's Way, with *The Lamb* at the north-western end of the ground adjacent to North Road. Both buildings are still there. It was the owner of *The Lamb*, one Thomas Norris, who had offered the ground to the Middlesex

George (aged 40) with his wife Mary and children (l to r from back) G.G., Rose, Ada, Frank and Alec.

George with sons G.G., Alec and Frank in Kent caps.

George (c. 1900) in his seventies.

Club. The neighbourhood was dominated by the very tall clock tower in the centre of the cattle market, which has been preserved. There were animal lairs or stalls along the southern side of Market Road, with a large fountain facing the clock tower whilst opposite, along North Road, two large hotels (now Queen's Mansions and City Mansions) were later separated by the Drovers Hall in 1873. Two other inns were located at each corner of the western end of the market area; *The Lion* still stands at the junction with North Road, but *The Black Bull* has been demolished.

The North Eastern Railway Line ran in a deep cutting along the eastern boundary of the cricket ground, emerging from a tunnel near *The White Horse*. The land sloped towards the narrow end of the site as noted by Thomas Case; this feature is confirmed by Marjorie Edwards, who has written a lively book of the old days entitled *"Up the Cally"* in which she gives a vivid description of life in the neighbourhood of the market, including the accounts which many people have given her about the struggle to push loaded carts and trolleys up the steep gradient to the market. This, then, was the cricket ground which held such an important place in the history of the Middlesex County Cricket Club, and of the two early Hearnes; it was the place where both men achieved some of their best performances.

George was appointed 'ground man' in 1864 at the new home of the Middlesex Club. Together with four other professional bowlers, he was available to members for practice; the professionals were not usually reckoned to be a regular part of the match team although both George Hearne and one other of the professional bowlers, W. Catling, took part in the historic match at the new ground on the 6th and 7th June 1864, when Middlesex played (and comfortably beat) a strong Sussex team containing two members of another great cricketing family, the Lillywhites, Charles Payne, one of the best batsmen of his day who seems to have turned out for Sussex or Kent as the fancy took him, and the 'super-itinerant' James Southerton. The latter actually played for three counties – Hampshire, Sussex and Surrey – in the same season and is reputed to have said he would have played for Kent too if they had been prepared to pay him. Like Cooper, James Lillywhite junior and Southerton were destined to appear in the first ever Test Match.

As already mentioned, both George and Thomas Hearne had played for Buckinghamshire, although in this match they were selected for Middlesex. Other Middlesex players in the side had more questionable connections with the home team and this upset some of the sports writers, who made known their objections to the choice of players with great force.

In this first year at Islington George made his best score of 72 for

Middlesex against MCC and Ground, an innings which included a hit for eight runs. It must be remembered that boundaries as we know them today were unknown until the 1860's when they were slowly introduced, so a big hit could be well rewarded.

George also achieved some good scores for Southgate, notably 48 against Surrey Club and Ground in 1863, out of a total of 494, which was easily the club's highest score since its foundation. This total was eclipsed in 1867 when Southgate played the Free Foresters and scored 508 with George this time making 73.

In 1865 George was employed by John Walker, who had provided a cricket ground at Southgate, mainly to coach the local village cricketers. It is possible that he had begun to see that his employment at Islington did not hold any great future prospects in view of the uneasy relationship between Thomas Norris, the owner of the ground, and the Middlesex Club, and he may have felt he had to obtain a more secure job. In the event the arrangement with Walker lasted a satisfactory and happy eight years.

In 1868 George Hearne scored 14 not out and 9 in his last match for Middlesex, who beat Yorkshire at Islington. With his future now more secure, George with his wife and five children moved to Southgate in 1867 where the youngest child, Randolph, was born in 1870. They lived almost adjacent to the northern boundary of the cricket ground; the address in the 1871 census is described as 'Lodge in Field', adjoining Blue Row (now Balaams Lane on the west side of Southgate High Street).

One of George's early major tasks at Southgate in 1867 was to re-lay the pitch and he relates that a 'so-called authority' on pitches reported un-favourably on his work. V.E. and I.D. Walker came to see him in a state of some disquiet but he was not in the least upset and reckoned that as neither gentleman had scored a century on the ground up until then, they would now do so on his new pitch. He went so far as to bet a week's wages that he would be proved right. His confidence was justified as V.E. made 138 and I.D. 107 against the Free Foresters in the second match on the newly-laid pitch.

Big matches at Southgate were a social event in those early days. Arnos Grove House, home of the Walkers, would be full of guests with many tents erected on the cricket ground to accommodate both the gentry and their ladies and the local spectators who attended in very large numbers. The band of the Life Guards provided appropriate music for the enjoyment of all. The large house lay to the east of a very extensive area of fields and woods, with Christ Church to the North on Church Hill, and opposite the cricket ground, which is still the home of Southgate Cricket Club.

The family move to Southgate was to prove of great significance in later years, particularly to George's three elder sons, George (junior), Frank and Alec, who later played for Kent. Towards the early 1870s it became apparent that the reign of the Walkers was drawing to a close as only a few matches were being played on the Southgate ground, so, after all the happy years he and his family had spent there, George was once again faced with the possibility of having to seek another post in the cricket world. Good fortune was once more on his side as when he was playing for Southgate at Upton Park he was approached by Mr. Hoare (later Sir Samuel Hoare, Bart., M.P.) who was well aware of George's excellent abilities as a groundsman. Hoare was looking for someone to take charge of the Private Banks Ground at Catford and offered him the job, which he accepted after seeking agreement from Walker, which was readily forthcoming. George maintained his situation at the Private Banks ground until a short time before his death at the end of 1904.

In *The Walkers of Southgate* there is a short chapter relating the reminiscences of Samuel Hoare in which he recalls being at school with 'Russy' Walker, whilst 'Donny' Walker went to the same school later. John Walker was a great friend of Sir Samuel although he was considerably the elder, and it was due to this close friendship that he allowed his old professional, George Hearne to become ground-man at Catford Bridge. Hoare remarks that this turned out such a fortunate thing for the ground; it was also an exceedingly great stroke of luck for George and his family as time was to show.

The family eventually moved to Catford Bridge and when the boys grew up they lived in Canadian Avenue (formerly Berlin Road but renamed in World War I), Broomhill Road and other nearby streets.

The district now occupied by Brownhill Road and other adjoining roads was formerly part of the farmland of North Park Farmhouse in Duncrievie Road, near where Hither Green railway station is now located. In the middle of the 18th century a large wood of some 40 acres known as Butlers Gardens occupied the ground where Hither Green Lane joins Brownhill Road. This portion of Brownhill Road was made in 1883 when building operations began.

The growth of Lewisham and district in the 19th and 20th centuries was similar to that of many London suburbs. The attractiveness of the area and the fact that it was within easy reach of London resulted in increasing numbers of middle-class families erecting houses with spacious gardens. With the building of the railway, land development and population growth accelerated enormously.

It still remains a puzzle why the Walkers did not foresee that George's sons would soon become qualified to play for Kent by virtue of residence there. They would have seen the youngsters growing up and developing into promising young cricketers who might well have played for Middlesex, as Lord Harris conceded when he approached George's father for the lads' service with Kent a few years later.

The question must be asked whether Middlesex actually wanted more than a very few professional players in their sides of this period; the teams were selected from a majority of amateurs up to the early 20th century. In 1901, for example, only three professionals, J.T. Hearne, Trott, and Rawlin played for the side. If this was the case, then clearly the Walkers would not have worried too much over the professional element in the 1870s. It is interesting to note that in the Middlesex Colts match of 1875, played at Prince's Ground, the Colts side comprised eleven amateurs, five professionals and the organiser Charles Absolon. This might suggest that the club was not seriously seeking professional talent. At that time they could not have foreseen the possibility of a shortage of public school and university amateurs within the large catchment area of London.

George Hearne soon relaid the Catford wicket as he found the subsoil was very damp and became waterlogged and even flooded by the adjacent River Ravensbourne in a bad winter. With his improvements, it was possible for first class matches to take place on occasions when play was impossible at Lord's and the Oval. He always felt that if more top grade cricket had been played there, resources would have been available to make the wicket comparable with any in the land.

George was a very useful cricketer; as a batsman he could be relied upon to keep his end up when wickets were falling and to hit out effectively if quick runs were wanted. He was not considered a bowler but could keep wicket very skilfully if required. A fine deep fieldsman, he was also an excellent long stop, a very important field placement in those early days of indifferent and bumpy pitches and probably erratic bowling also. He did not achieve anything like the performances of his brother Thomas and he might have compared much more favourably if he had devoted more of his time to playing and less to his various other pursuits.

Middlesex was not the only prominent team for which George played. He appeared for Clarke's All England Eleven, the United South of England and Wisden and Dean's United All England Eleven. He is also reported to have taken part in the solitary match that the New United South of England Eleven played in 1875.

Although no records have come to light of his performances for any of the other teams mentioned above, there are several known instances of his scores for and against the United All England Eleven. On 7, 8 and 9 August 1862 George and his brother Thomas were in the Sixteen of Southgate v. United All England match at Southgate, when the Sixteen gained a comfortable victory by an innings and forty-two runs. Thomas made 24 and George was undefeated on 20. Whilst George appears to have been 'loyal' to the local club, Thomas played for whichever of the teams required his services for this annual match.

The following year, on 6, 7 and 8 August 1863 the United All England side played at Southgate for the last time and were trounced by an innings and sixty-five runs, the brothers Hearne playing on opposite sides.

In later life, whilst recounting some of the early matches when the brothers played on opposite sides, nothing pleased George more than to describe in his inimitable manner the matches in which his side was victorious over the side containing Tom. Tradition has it that this was wont to cause old Thomas to growl as he did not share his brother's sense of humour. According to the author's grandparents, these moods matched his appearance.

George Hearne was a very genial man, and everyone who knew him held him in high esteem. He was an affectionate family man who was understandably proud of his cricketing sons and always ready to talk about them. His fondness for a good yarn has already been mentioned and the following were among his favourite stories:-

Of one of his Middlesex matches George says, "I was batting against Notts at the Old Cattle Market at Islington; Mr. I.D. Walker was at the other end, and Biddulph at the wicket. In the course of my innings, I played a ball hard into my pads, and couldn't get it out. So I ran round the wicket, and Biddulph after me, bustling me at every step. I tried everything I could think of, using the handle of my bat to force the ball out, and hitting the pad with the bat, but Biddulph kept so close that it seemed ages before I managed to poke out the ball. Then a good deal to my surprise the bowler asked, 'How's that?' and the umpire said, 'Out!' Mr. Walker promptly turned round and said 'Out! What for?' The umpire said, 'Leg before wicket'. 'How on earth can that be'. asked Mr. Walker. 'Why he hit the ball into his pad'. 'Well', said the umpire, 'I've given him out anyway, and he's got to go'. 'But what for?' asked Mr. Walker. 'Well', said the umpire slowly, 'for handling ball'. And I had to go out".

On another occasion, in a village match, old George was the victim of an umpire. "I went in first", he said, "with Mr. Walter Street, and after we had been in for a little while I overheard one of the players say to the umpire –

their umpire, of course – 'There's only these two Hearnes (my brother Tom was also playing), and if we can get them out we're all right'. The umpire said nothing, but a few minutes afterwards I was given out in a shocking manner, lbw. Mr. Street was very indignant, and said, 'If this happens again I shall take my team off the field as a protest'. When I got to the pavilion I said to my brother Tom, who was to go in next, 'They'll have you for certain'. After he had made seven or eight runs, a ball hit him on the leg, and he was promptly given out – an even worse decision than in my own case. Mr. Street said, 'Come on, Tom, we'll have no more of this. We'll go home and have a hit there'. And we went home at once".

"I was once given out at Taplow lbw to a ball which hit me under the chin, when I was standing nearly upright. It was a pretty bad wicket, and during my innings another ball hit me on the head and went for three byes. I remember a curious case in which the two umpires differed. It was in a match between Ealing and Twickenham. A ball was hit into a cedar tree, which was not regarded as a boundary, and lodged on one of the branches. One of the Parsons of Ealing ran for the ball and pulled off his boot to throw at it, eventually succeeding in knocking it down. Meanwhile we had been running, and when the ball was thrown in at last we had run twelve. One umpire said that it was lost ball and that six ought to be counted; the other umpire couldn't see this, for he said that as the tree was not a boundary, and as the ball was in sight all the time it couldn't be lost. In the end it was agreed that we were only to count six. Talking of boundaries reminds me that when I was a boy I was playing at the Windsor Barracks for the Hearne family eleven, where the ground was not very big. A ball which was hit hard against the wall rebounded to me and I brought off a catch. I thought I had done something very clever, and was a good deal astonished and disgusted when I found that the man still continued to bat".

Fate was to deal George Hearne a cruel blow for he developed a dreadful, malignant internal growth. At the age of 75, on 9th December 1904, this hitherto happy and jovial man met a very painful end at 41 Rosenthal Road, Catford, the home of his eldest son, leaving behind a grief-stricken family.

Chapter 6

George Gibbons Hearne
(Kent 1875-1895)

THROUGHOUT the history of cricket there are sons who have followed in the footsteps of their fathers, but few have eclipsed the fame of their seniors. It is therefore surprising that 'Old George' Hearne had three sons who all became excellent first class players performing to a much higher standard than their father.

George Gibbons Hearne, eldest of the triumvirate, was born on July 7th 1856 at Hornton Cottages, Uxbridge Road, Ealing Dean (now West Ealing). Early portraits show him as a plump youngster with a chubby face, an unusual characteristic for a Hearne cricketer. He was coached by his father and Uncle Thomas on the local cricket ground behind *The Green Man*.

When a small boy he did not lack courage or application when his side was in trouble. In one match for Southgate against Winchmore Hill, his father, as captain of the local side, had put himself low down the batting order. Evidently 'Old George' had endured a thirsty day in the field and felt he needed a cup of home brewed tea before batting and nipped off to his nearby cottage for a quick one. Alas, he had hardly finished his first cup before a hot and perspiring youth arrived short of breath and panting out that the Village were five for six wickets! By the time George had covered the short sprint from home eight wickets had fallen, and he found his young son – George – still at the crease cool and collected, keeping his end up to such good effect that the lad went on to make 73 not out whilst his senior partner scored 54 to win the match.

Young George was showing greater promise at the age of 17 in 1873 when he scored a splendid 78 not out whilst playing for Sixteen Young Players of Middlesex against Eleven of the County on Paige's Ground at Holloway for Abel Kidd's benefit. He had already impressed the Walker brothers who seemingly had considered him a potential Middlesex player while he was in his early teens and had encouraged his play as an all-rounder.

Even earlier, when only 12 or 13 years old, he played for the Boys of Southgate against the Boys of Cockfosters with his younger brother Frank. George had made 102 and Frank 85 when their opponents pulled up the stumps and made off having made it clear that they had had enough.

By 1875 'Old George' and his family had lived at Catford for two years and his eldest son's ability as a cricketer had improved all the while. Lord Harris, the power behind Kent County Cricket Club, visited the ground that year to inspect the wicket which George had prepared for a Colts match to be played on 4th and 5th of May. One of his distinguished friends suggested it would be a good idea to get some net practice whilst they were there. Lord Harris was surprised to see a young boy with the ball instead of 'Old George' and he was even more surprised when the youth hit his stumps a few times. Georgie always said he thought the noble lord had allowed himself to be bowled as encouragement; however Lord Harris was so impressed that he immediately suggested that the youngster should play in the Colts game. Some thought he was too young and it was also pointed out that V.E. Walker required him for Middlesex. His lordship waived the first objection, saying that it would not do the lad any harm, so young George played and displayed a form far above his fellow fifteen team-mates against a County Eleven. From then on he was a county player for Kent, and not for Middlesex which would have seemed more likely. Lord Harris's account of the matter suggests that there was no documentary evidence of the arrangement, simply an honourable understanding, and he writes:-

"Old George Hearne had just completed two years as a groundsman at Catford Bridge, lent to Kent County Cricket Club by the Private Banks Club. Young George Gibbons was thus qualified to play for Kent under residential qualification and fancying I foresaw his merits I made a bargain with his father that if I played the boy for the County he should stick to us. So if I lost Harry Wood I found in the young Hearne and his brothers a goldmine, for most likely the Walkers would have secured their services for Middlesex for which County they were qualified to play by birth".

What the Walkers really thought will never be known and as there is no family account of the 'bargain', the real truth of the matter must remain a subject of speculation.

George Gibbons played his first match at Lord's on 10th May 1875 in a twelve-a-side match for the Colts of the South, captained by Lord Harris, against the Colts of the North, captained by A. Shrewsbury. Young George only managed 1 and 0 with the bat but took 3 wickets for 24 runs.

On 21st June 1875 G.G., as he eventually became known, was afforded another opportunity to test his merits, this time for Kent against Derbyshire at Derby. He did not achieve outstanding figures in these two early matches but showed his real potential a little later against Lancashire at Old Trafford when

Kent 1888   *back: W.Wright, F.Marchant, C.J.M.Fox, F.Martin*
centre: W.Rashleigh, W.H.Patterson, Lord Harris, M.C.Kemp
front: A.Hearne, G.G.Hearne, F.Hearne

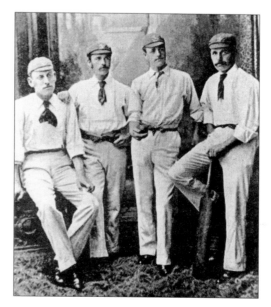

l to r:
Walter, Alec, Frank and
George Gibbons Hearne

he took eight wickets for forty-six runs, including the hat trick, and four for nine against Hampshire at Winchester.

He finished his first season for Kent with 28 wickets at an average of under 10, over half being clean bowled. He bowled with a round-arm delivery – left-handed – at fast-medium pace. Many of his wickets were taken with balls which had a natural break and which provided the safe hands of C.A. Absolom with many catches in the slips.

G.G. immediately became a firm favourite with the Press who seemed to praise his efforts at almost any possible opportunity, referring to him variously as 'Wee George' or 'the little chap'. Wisden referred to him as ". . . the little pet of the press . . ." but rather overdid things themselves when recording Kent's heavy defeat by Derbyshire in 1875 by saying, "young George Hearne played steadily for some time for 0!"

About the time George Gibbons Hearne was introduced into the Kent County team he was living at Fern Villa, 35 Brownhill Road, which was a fairly new house. Later G.G. moved to 'Ty-bach', 41 Brownhill Road, Catford.

In 1876 he was engaged at Prince's ground, and during this season bowled with considerable success. His batting was improving with maturity, shown by an innings of 57 not out versus The Gentlemen of MCC at Canterbury when Kent amassed 473 and then dismissed their opponents for a meagre 144 in their first innings, G.G. taking 3 wickets in 4.1 overs for no runs. The amateurs' second knock was an entirely different matter. Following on 329 runs in arrears, on a scorching hot day, they thrashed the perspiring Kent bowlers, or at least the mighty W.G. Grace did, for 557 to make the match a memorable draw. W.G. made 344 in an innings lasting a little over six hours. This was a somewhat sobering experience for young G.G. who could only manage one wicket for 91 in this riot of runs. Other matches afforded him more rewards, including a convincing victory for Kent against Lancashire at Gravesend in August when he captured 7 second innings wickets for 43.

The following year he was appointed to the ground staff at Lord's where he was to remain engaged for nearly 25 years. As a result of the new opportunities now open to him, his all-round performances became even better. It was a season when his bowling for the County really took off with 105 wickets for 1,235 runs. This earned him the distinction of being the first man to take a hundred wickets in a season for Kent.

At Derby in June, Kent won an exciting match mainly due to G.G.'s fine bowling in both innings – 6 for 52 and 8 for 78. They were also victorious against Lancashire immediately afterwards at Old Trafford when George took 7 for 30 and 5 for 45.

Other fine bowling feats which took place that successful Kent season were George's 7 for 45 and 4 for 68 at Brighton against Sussex in July, where Kent won by 10 wickets, and 5 for 63 against Lancashire at Mote Park, Kent winning by one wicket.

During two days of the Tunbridge Wells Cricket Week George took 6 wickets in each of the Sussex innings for a total of 55 runs, and Wisden may have gone slightly overboard in their justifiable praise of his efforts when they said: "Pretty good 'County' work this for a 21-year-old, especially when it is borne in mind three of the wickets were bowled for 0, and that the little lad took his bat out for 25!"

George Gibbons' best innings that season were 121 not out for MCC and Ground v Cambridge, when he carried his bat, 81 at Winchester, and 121 not out for MCC and Ground against the Long Vacation Club at the end of the season. This same summer George first played for South v North.

In 1878 he was the only member of the Kent eleven to play in all fifteen of the County's matches, being the outstanding player of the season. He took 13 Hampshire wickets for 75 runs at Southampton in June. Then, during the Canterbury Week, young George distinguished himself in the match between Eleven of England and Thirteen of Kent by taking 3 wickets in each of the England innings, catching five of his opponents out and scoring 83 not out in a big stand with Lord Harris (93). His greatest prize in this match was getting the wicket (caught and bowled) of W.G. Grace for 21 and his excellent all-round cricket earned him a collection of over £20. In the next match during this beautiful cricket week, starting on the 'Ladies' Day', George more or less carried on from where he had left off by making 60 runs and bowling the mighty W.G. for a duck; not a happy match for the bearded warrior as A. Penn bowled him for a single in his second innings, which contributed to a Kent win by 9 wickets.

George was in the MCC team in May 1878 against the Australians at Lord's when the tourists really showed their capabilities for the future by bowling out the strong MCC side for a mere 33 and 19. Although the Australians only made 41 in the first innings they knocked off the few runs needed for a conclusive win in their second, for the loss of one wicket, thus completing the match in one day.

That season George showed good all-round form with a batting average of 20 but it was his bowling that really shone and he topped the Kent averages with 96 wickets. Among his best analyses were 13 for 75 in the match against Hampshire at Southampton; 5 for 49 against Nottinghamshire at Town Malling; 5 for 25 and 6 for 40 against Derbyshire at Mote Park, Maidstone;

and 5 for 73 against Lancashire at Town Malling. Kent were caught on a rain-affected wicket in the latter match, which they lost after following on.

Although G.G. did fairly well with both bat and ball for Kent in 1879, including 14 for 45 in the match against MCC and Ground at Lord's, he reserved most of his best performances for the occasions when he represented MCC. Against Essex at Brentwood he scored a fine 168 and took 9 wickets for 75 runs.

This pattern of solid all-round success for Kent and MCC and Ground was continued as the 1880s unfolded.

Meanwhile, on 12th March 1881, George Gibbons Hearne married Mary Jane Sharon of 32 Chancellor Road, now Chancellor Grove, Norwood, Lambeth. Her father Joseph Sharon had been a coachman and would have had a lot in common with his daughter's new father-in-law 'Old George' Hearne whom we know to have been very keen on horses himself. Although young George was by then a well-established professional cricketer, his marriage certificate describes both himself and his father as 'Contractors', possibly on account of their winter occupation of working on and preparing cricket grounds.

1884 saw the introduction to the County team of his younger brother Alec who was to prove an even greater asset than G.G. himself, and also the first appearance of their cousin Herbert Hearne. G.G.'s best scores for Kent were 116 and 61 against Hampshire at Gravesend when he and Lord Harris virtually ensured their side a victory.

1885 was not a very spectacular season for George Gibbons, but this year is noteworthy for the fact that all the four Hearnes who played for Kent appeared in the County averages, namely G.G., Frank and Alec, and Herbert. All four took part in the match at Tonbridge between the Players of Kent and the Gentlemen of Kent, which was hastily arranged because of the cancellation of the fixture with Lancashire resulting from the dispute over alleged throwing by the Lancashire bowlers John Crossland and George Nash.

Minor games in 1885 saw G.G. gather a strong side in April to play West Kent Wanderers at Blackheath for R. Ramsey's benefit; the side included 'G.G.', Frank, Alec and Herbert Hearne, F. Martin, J. Wootton, E. O'Shaughnessy, J.M. Read and H. Wood.

1886 was G.G.'s most successful season with the bat, and he led the Kent averages with 987 runs at an average of 41, his total in all first-class games that year being 1,125 runs. His most notable performance was 126 in the second innings against Middlesex at Gravesend when his brother Frank also scored a century and shared in a partnership of 226. He made 117 *v* Yorkshire at Canterbury, figuring in a stand of 215 with Cecil (later Bishop) Wilson, and 75 and 50 against Nottinghamshire at Maidstone when he also took 6 wickets for 34 runs. He also scored 53 *v* the Australians at Canterbury in August, a match which Kent won. G.G. also scored seven centuries in MCC and other matches.

Another cricket match on Easter Monday of 1886 was far less important but very successful for the Hearnes. No less than six of them appeared in G.G.'s team against Blackheath on Rectory Field. G.G. himself took 7 for 47 in the match and Alec took 7 for 40. Frank, Herbert, Walter, and George Francis also took part. The Blackheath team included S. Christopherson and M.J. Druitt, and the game was the first one to be played on the ground laid out by G.G.

The next year, 1887 (the year of Queen Victoria's Golden Jubilee), he was appointed captain of the Players of the South *v* the Players of the North at Beckenham when he made a top score of 67 on an indifferent wicket and his side won by 5 wickets. He also took part in the MCC Centenary match at Lord's, scoring only 8 and 6 for MCC who were defeated overwhelmingly by England.

Unfortunately later that month he sprained an ankle whilst playing for Kent *v* Notts and was not able to play again that season. Even so he averaged 25 with the bat in first-class matches.

Ill luck dogged him in 1888, which was a wretchedly wet summer, and he caught a form of fever by refusing to take medical precautions after a very bad cold when he felt he should carry on playing. Eventually he was so ill he was forced to take a rest.

George Gibbons Hearne's main score in 1889 was 103 for Kent *v* Sussex and 64 not out for the County *v* Yorkshire. Also in that year he made three separate centuries for the MCC and Ground.

1889 also saw the last match in which Lord Harris captained the Kent County Cricket team, as he had been appointed Governor of Bombay and left for India the following spring. Fate decreed that it should be a very important game for Kent, for if their opponents, Nottinghamshire, were victorious they would become champions; if on the other hand Kent won then Notts would only be on level terms with both Surrey and Lancashire.

After a good start on the difficult Beckenham wicket the home county had to struggle for runs as the pitch deteriorated. At the end of their first innings they had made a total of 118, chasing a Notts first innings of 134. Following a start of 24 for 2 Notts' were all out for 35 in their second knock leaving Kent a mere 52 runs to win. But those runs had to be made on a really treacherous

Yours truly
Geo. G. Hearne

wicket and soon 6 wickets were lost for 25. However the imperturbable George Gibbons remained at the crease and the game was won by 4 wickets. Attewell for Notts took 4 of the 6 wickets for 7 runs with 21 maidens out of the 25 overs he bowled, some indication of the conditions. There was however, one sad aspect of this exciting event for it was the match in which G.G.'s young brother Frank played his last game for the County before leaving for South Africa.

1890 was not a distinguished year for George as he scored less than 500 runs for Kent and took only 4 wickets. Since he was possibly apprehensive of the future due to several seasons of poor overall performances, he established a sports shop in Lewisham. He was also granted a benefit during Canterbury Week which raised £511 19s 0d. The match chosen was against Surrey who participated in the Week for the first time. Several distinguished former amateur players, including three past or future presidents, George Marsham, F.A. MacKinnon and W.H. Patterson, took a collection on the first day.

The next two years did not go at all well for Kent; poor fielding and wet Augusts did not help. 1892 was a particularly bad season as the County only won two matches and shared the bottom of the table with Gloucestershire. G.G. managed a batting average of 21.70 for Kent but was eclipsed by his brother Alec with an average for the County of 32.18.

In 1891-92 W.W. Read's touring side visiting South Africa included three Hearne's, G.G. and Alec of Kent and J.T. of Middlesex. It must be said that of the trio G.G. did the least to distinguish himself.

The party sailed in the Dunottar Castle to Cape Town where they arrived on 8th December. Numerous provincial matches were played in which the visitors' bowling proved too good for the home sides. In fact there was only one eleven-a-side match played on 19th, 21st and 22nd March at Cape Town and it is now considered a Test Match. England were far too strong for their opponents and won easily by an innings and 189 runs, the interesting feature being the appearance of four Hearnes, three for England (two brothers and a cousin) and one for South Africa (the third brother).

After having been a member of the MCC ground staff for twenty-one years George Gibbons Hearne was awarded a benefit at Lord's in May-June 1898. One more big score in his career was added in 1899. When playing for the MCC and Ground v Plymouth Garrison at Mount Wise, he and H.F. Brunshill added 200 for the last wicket; G.G. made 125 and his partner was 57 not out.

George Gibbons Hearne, together with his two cricketer brothers, had the good fortune to have the interest of Lord Harris at the times which were critical for their development into first-class players. 'G.G.' in particular blossomed under Lord Harris's leadership and the latter took care not to over-bowl his young protégé.

He was a fine fieldsman and a left-hand batsman difficult to remove once he was well set, driving and cutting brilliantly. He would have made more large scores if Lord Harris had not run him out so often, a fact his lordship readily admitted, adding that "George was always ready to go".

An even-tempered and humorous man, he was an expert at laying out cricket grounds, including the Oxford University Ground, the Gloucestershire County Ground at Bristol, one on the Ballaggio Estate at East Grinstead, Rectory Field, Blackheath and the Crabble Ground, Dover, with his brother Alec. This is not surprising in view of the vast experience gained from his father and Uncle Thomas. He coached at Marlborough and other public schools at various times.

G.G.'s sports business at 140 Lewisham High Road, which was eventually demolished in 1913 to make way for Deptford Library, rapidly became a well-known establishment and was advertised in the summer issues of *Cricket. A Weekly Record of the Game.*

His best-known product was the 'Quick Spring' bat, made on the premises under his personal supervision. Stock included all the accessories for cricket, football and lawn tennis, and it all added up to a thriving home and export market. Among the overseas customers was his brother Frank in South Africa.

In about 1883 G.G. became a founder of Catford Cricket Club, who initially played in the area now occupied by Culverley Road. He remained devoted to cricket, especially to his local team, and he even turned out a few times in his advanced years whilst living at Rosenthal Road.

The cricket outfitting activities carried on at 140 Lewisham High Road were transferred to Messrs Wisden of Cranbourne Street in approximately 1895, as George found that he could not manage the whole of his business any longer due to his many engagements.

His last noteworthy match took place during the First World War when he played in a charity game arranged by his club, at which W.G. Grace was present but not well enough to play, although he was active enough to go round the ground collecting money for the Belgian refugees who had fled from the German invaders.

George Gibbons' wife died in 1916 and eventually he resided at 56 Verdant Lane, Catford, with his unmarried daughter Mabel, until in 1932 he died after a long bout of bronchitis and influenza in King's College Hospital, Denmark Hill, aged 76.

Chapter 7

Frank Hearne
(Kent 1879-89. W. Province 1890/1-1903/4)

THE second of 'old George' Hearne's sons, Frank, was born at their Ealing home opposite *The Green Man* on the Uxbridge Road on 23rd November 1858. He was the middle boy in the trio of brothers whose all round cricket ability was to serve Kent County Cricket Club for many years. When only six years old his father took over the care of the Walker brothers' cricket pitch at Southgate, consequently the family moved into a cottage adjacent to the northern boundary of the ground.

All three brothers were small men, Frank, the shortest, being only 5 feet 5 inches tall, but this proved to be no impediment to a long and distinguished career. He became a fine all round cricketer with a sound defence coupled with strong off side strokes; a right-handed round-arm change bowler he was also one of the most brilliant cover point fieldsmen of his time.

As a very young boy he first became interested in cricket at the ground his father and his Uncle Thomas had created behind *The Green Man* and there was plenty of scope for small boys to knock a ball about in the open fields behind his home.

Frank's first recorded score was during a game for Southgate School against Colney Hatch School; he was only thirteen years old at the time but made 70 not out, brother George was not out on 90 when their thoroughly disheartened opponents, despairing of ever getting a wicket, gave up the unequal contest. Twelve months later the family was again uprooted, this time to Catford, as the boy's father was appointed groundsman at the Private Banks Cricket Ground, Catford Bridge, Kent.

In 1875 Frank was employed as a ground bowler by the Private Banks Club, a position he retained until 1879 when he played for the Colts of Kent against the Colts of Surrey at Mote Park, Maidstone on 26th and 27th May. He immediately created a good impression by scoring a well made 33 and by some first class fielding, so much so that he was selected for Kent in their first match of the year against the MCC and Ground at Lord's on 12th June.

Most first class cricketers have their initial big match innings indelibly imprinted on their memory, but none could be more clear or more disasterous than that of poor Frank Hearne as he collected a duck in each innings; in his defence it must be said that his first innings run out was not his fault. He had opened the batting with his brother George and, although the latter did only marginally better than Frank with the bat, at least he collected a total of 14 wickets for 45 runs. In spite of this performance the MCC & Ground won by 50 runs, so it is not surprising to learn that in addition to Frank's 'pair' the last three Kent batsmen also failed to score in both innings.

Unlike some other members of the Hearne fraternity Frank's early career did not commence in a blaze of success. Indeed, his first seasons with the bat were, to say the least, very poor, but so brilliant was his fielding, far above the average seen in his day, that this alone secured him a place in the County side and he was also beginning to take a few wickets. However, it did seem at one stage that he might not make his way as a first class player for, in addition to indifferent scores, 1882 saw him suffer a severe blow on the head whilst playing against Yorkshire at Gravesend in August. The bowler, Ulyett, was unable to bring himself to bowl again in the match having, as he said, ". . nearly killed little Frankie".

His form began to improve steadily that season when he was engaged at Lord's, and the next year he only missed playing in two of the eighteen Kent County Club games. The 1884 summer saw one of the highlights in Frank's career when he and Lord Harris put on 89 runs in Kent's second innings against the Australians. Frank's score of 45 out of his sides' total of 213, together with his brother Alec's bowling, was a major contribution in the team's victory, which was the only match the tourists lost to a County side that year.

On 3rd October 1885 Frank Hearne, who was living at 16 Blythe Vale, Catford, married Rosa Lilley Howes at St. George's Church, Perry Hill, Lewisham. Rosa, aged 23, was from Blackheath where her late father William Howes had been a carpenter. Frank's father, George Hearne, is described on the marriage certificate as "Manager of the Banks Cricket Ground". Cousin Herbert Hearne and sister Ada Matilda Hearne were witnesses. Frank and Rosa later had three sons, of whom more later.

Together with his brother George Gibbons (G.G.), Frank was among the players most relied upon in the Kent XI in 1885. Both brothers played nineteen innings for the County, three more than anyone else, and at the end of the season only three runs separated their totals. Frank scored 377 and G.G. made 374, but as Frank had enjoyed two not outs to his brother's one he had the better average.

Frank Hearne

By now Frank and his elder brother George were becoming an important part of their County's batting strength, and they made some excellent scores. For instance, in a high-scoring match against Middlesex at Gravesend in 1886, they shared a partnership of 226 for Kent's second wicket, both making centuries.

Kent *v* Middlesex

Gravesend, 12, 13, 14 August 1886

Match drawn

KENT

First innings		Second innings	
F. Hearne c Dauglish b Webbe	47	c Burton b Robertson	142
Mr. W.H. Patterson b Burton	3	c Dauglish b Robertson	12
G.G. Hearne b Robertson	53	b Robertson	126
Lord Harris c Stoddart b Burton	27	b Webbe	76
Mr. M.C.Kemp b Robertson	10	b Webbe	0
Mr. A.J.Thornton not out	25	not out	0
Rev. R.T. Thornton, b Robertson	3		
Mr. F. Marchant c West b Burton	0		
Hickmott b Robertson	0		
Wootton c Robertson b Burton	13		
Herbert Hearne c Robertson b Burton	6		
Extras	9		18
	196	(for 5 wickets)	**374**

MIDDLESEX

Mr. A.J. Webbe c A.J. Thornton b F. Hearne	103	Mr. F.G.J. Ford b Marchant	0
Mr. A.E.Stoddart, run out	116	Mr. M.J. Dauglish b Wootton	1
Mr. S.W. Scott c R.T. Thornton b Wootton	30	Mr. J. Robertson c Marchant b G. Hearne	3
Mr. J.G. Walker c H. Hearne b Wooton	79	Burton c Harris b A.J. Thornton	25
Spillman c Marchant b Wootton	0	B 5, 1-b 2, w 1	8
Mr. T.C. O'Brien not out	88		
West run out	4		**457**

MIDDLESEX BOWLING

	Overs	Mdns.	Runs	Wkts.	Overs	Mdns.	Runs	Wkts.
Burton	48.2	25	56	5	62	35	65	0
Mr. Robertson	32	12	58	4	53.2	16	108	3
West	6	2	13	0	25	18	52	0
Mr. Ford	8	3	20	0	27	14	35	0
Mr. Webbe	18	5	40	1	49	30	52	2
Mr. Stoddart					12	4	27	0
Mr. Dauglish					3	1	13	0
Mr. Walker					1	0	4	0

KENT BOWLING

	Overs	Mdns.	Runs	Wkts.		Overs	Mdns.	Runs	Wkts.
Wootton	85	31	123	4	Rev. R.T. Thornton	4	1	18	0
H. Hearne	28	5	75	0	Mr. Patterson	5	0	16	0
G.G. Hearne	39	18	61	1	F. Hearne	17	4	48	1
Mr. A.J. Thornton	30.3	8	66	1	Mr. Marchant	10	3	28	1
Lord Harris	6	0	14	0					

Kent's second innings, to paraphrase Wisden was the most sensational part of the match, George and Frank Hearne, whose maiden first-class century this was, obtaining a complete mastery over the weak bowling. Although the match inevitably ended in a draw, there was a collection on behalf of Frank and G.G. which resulted in over £12 being donated by the appreciative crowd.

That same year Frank played one of his greatest innings, 111 for the South of England in a drawn match against Australia, also at Gravesend, on 30th and 31st August and 1st September. Both Frank and Maurice Read had only made 13 runs between them in the South's first innings total of 170, to which the Australians replied with 299. The South's second knock was a different matter and they amassed 450 runs, thanks mainly to a brilliant stand of 191 between Frank and Read; both eventually fell to Spofforth, Frank for 111 and Read for 109.

Between 1879 and 1889 Frank Hearne played 127 matches for Kent, scoring 3,426 runs and taking 41 wickets, one of his outstanding scores being 144 against Yorkshire in 1887. Consistently good performances saw Frank included in Major R.G. Warton's team to tour South Africa in 1888-89. C.A. Smith of Sussex, the captain of the side, was later to become better known as Sir C. Aubrey Smith, the actor and film star.

Frank journeyed to South Africa a few weeks before his fellow English cricketers, probably in order to get really fit and well for the forthcoming tour and to do some coaching. His early arrival was greeted with some misgivings by the local Press who seemed to think that he had been sent out as a special agent to run an expert eye over future opponents of the English and report their strengths and weaknesses to his captain on the latter's subsequent arrival. Apparently the Cape Town cricketers would have nothing to do with such nonsense and considered that a week's coaching from Frank would be of benefit to them; however, the newspapers thought that he would learn as much as he taught ". . unless precautions are taken". One wonders what exactly they had in mind.

On arrival in South Africa Frank Hearne did not waste much time before appearing in his first game when he played for Western Province against Claremont, making 77 and taking 3 wickets, a creditable performance for one who had never before played on a matting wicket and had hardly found his legs after the long sea voyage.

The main body of the English touring side sailed aboard the Castle Packet Company's 3,705 tons *Garth Castle*, calling at Lisbon and Madeira and landing at Cape Town on 14th December.

The tour of South Africa was enjoyed immensely by Frank Hearne, who

A 'Colonial Frank' in South Africa.

Grandson Lionel displaying some of Frank's trophies.

At their Cape home, Frank with sons George (left) and Frank junior.

played in nearly all of the games, and although he did not achieve anything spectacular there is no doubt that it was beneficial for his health, for there appears to be no mention of any major ailments until he was quite aged.

To say that travelling in those days was primitive is no overstatement, and for some of the time it was positively dangerous. On one occasion Bobby Abel was convinced that his last day (or night, in fact) had come, as the cart he was in got lost, and he had to be suitably fortified the next day before he could be compelled to cross the turbulent Oliphant river. The hardships endured did not worry Frank in the least, and his cousin J.T. Hearne who toured the same areas a few years later positively revelled in the hazardous conditions.

Frank seems to have borne the various injuries suffered in his playing days with remarkable composure. For instance, one of the few games which Warton's team lost was against a Cape Colony XI who defeated them easily by 10 wickets. Frank was bowled for 17 by Vintcent in the first innings, and in the second knock he received a bad blow to his hand from Theunissen just before lunch. During the interval he underwent surgical treatment and despite the suffering from his crushed fingers he resumed his innings after the break, being cheered to the wicket by the crowd, who encouraged him to go on and score 41 not out.

Some of the tour matches were very one-sided and must have been quite hilarious. For example, in a game against Pietermaritzburg Districts XXII the locals in their second innings managed 69 runs out of which only two batsmen got into double figures, and there were ten ducks excluding the last man not out 0! This was surpassed by a Cape Rifles XXII when no batsman achieved double figures out of a total of 39, thirteen failing to score at all. Their second effort was marginally better as one batsman made 17 out of 54 and there were only 12 ducks. Needless to say, these slaughters provided the English bowlers with some quite extraordinary returns. Briggs and Fothergill wrought havoc in the match with Midland Districts XXII who managed totals of 109 and 45 (one double figure score of 14 and no less than 14 ducks). Briggs finished the match with 21 wickets for 48 runs and Fothergill 14-42.

Whilst the 2 Tests were not as farcical as these encounters, they still resulted in overwhelming victories for the tourists.

This brief account of the first English cricket side to tour South Africa cannot be concluded without mention of a remarkable coincidence. The Author had just written the draft account of the farewell to the tourists and of the presentation to each of the members of a gold shield as a souvenir of the visit when a letter was received from Raymond Hearne of Fish Hoek, a grandson of Frank Hearne, containing a cutting from the Port Elizabeth

Weekend Post of Saturday 8th February 1992 illustrating this very medal which had just been discovered in a pawnbroker's, where it had been lying in an old box full of odds and ends. The 18-carat medallion has three stumps on the face, crossed by two cricket bats and two cricket balls, and two scrolls read "Port Elizabeth" and "1889". The reverse reads F. HEARNE 1889.

Although the South African tour was successful from a playing point of view, the financial situation left much to be desired; this was however not the fault of the players, who returned home on 16th April in the *Garth Castle*.

Frank Hearne's last game for Kent CCC was against Nottinghamshire on 29th and 30th August 1889 at Beckenham, the last match of the season. Coincidentally it was also Lord Harris' last game for Kent, and, as described in the previous chapter, the game that decided the championship. Frank had a quiet game, although G.G.'s stubborn batting won Kent the game.

A hint that Frank Hearne was suffering failing health appears in *Wisden's* account of this match when it states that he was compelled to leave England for a warmer climate. During the luncheon break on the second day's play the Kent CCC President, Mr. F.A. MacKinnon, presented him with £144 9s 10d, collected by his colleagues, and Lord Harris added his praise of Frank's character both as a man and as a fellow cricketer.

An earlier comment that all was not well with Frank's health had appeared in the September 1888 issue of *Cricket* when mention was made that "Major Warton, who is going to personally conduct the team of English cricketers to the Cape, has been able to include Frank Hearne . . . and the trip, with the change of climate, and above all the sea voyage, should be the means of setting him up thoroughly again . . ." This was an opinion that was fully justified in the ensuing years.

Most writers, including Wisden, state that he was obliged to emigrate due to ill-health. However, in the March 1989 issue of *The Cricketer International*, Gerald Howat writes that Western Province offered Frank a five-year contract as their professional at a salary of £150 with a free house, rates and annual benefit, with the responsibility in winter months for the nearby Rugby Union Ground. It is unfortunate that family legend does not record which reason for his emigration was the real one, and it could have been a combination of various factors which induced the move. One thing is certain; he did not stay in South Africa on account of the gold rush, like some cricketers. It is significant that he played for the Western Province Cricket Club from 1889/90 to 1903/4 and lived to the age of 91, so it seems that his health was reasonably sound. His connection with Western Province C.C. may well have been influenced by the fact that Major Warton himself had been a member of Western Province C.C. since 1883 when he was posted to the Army General Staff in the Cape.

As a final gesture of appreciation of Frank's loyal and successful career with Kent, a benefit on his behalf was played against the Forest Hill Club on their ground when eighteen of their members met Frank Hearne's XI. Lord Harris acted as the captain of Frank's XI which had the best of the encounter, the captain and Maurice Read putting on 147 for the third wicket. Going in for a second time 120 runs behind, the Eighteen were 21 for 7 at the close of play.

After the match, during which a collection yielded £25 for the benefit fund, a dinner was given in the grounds of the Rutland Hotel on Penny Hill at which there were nearly 100 guests.

It is not known precisely when cricket began in Western Province, but it is said to have been played in the early 1850's at the Diocesan College and at military and naval stations at the Cape. Of these early matches, one was recorded as having taken place in January 1862 between Mother Country and Colonial Born, the latter winning by six wickets. As in England, the players did not confine themselves to one club; matches were played on bare grass until, in 1879, the Western Province Club apparently decided that bowlers were having too much of a good thing and introduced matting for use late in the season when the natural pitches became virtually unplayable. The Western Province Club was founded in 1864 and soon afterwards they moved from Rondesbosch to Higg's Field and then to Southey's Field, Wynberg, and finally to the Newlands ground in 1888. Matches here became the centre of important social gatherings and must have been even more impressive than the great days of the Walker brothers' big games at Southgate, for a military band played in front of the Governor, military chiefs and other important dignitaries who had come to watch the cricket. Western Province showed excellent judgement in their choice of Frank Hearne for, apart from the effect he soon had as a bowler and batsman, it soon became apparent that he was by far a better coach than the other Englishmen, Brockwell, Firkin and Mills. It can be said that the subsequent success of Western Province cricket was largely due to his influence, particularly the improvement he brought about in the younger generation of players.

Frank's initial game as a member of the Western Province Club was against Natal in January 1890 in a friendly match when he scored 0 and 58. Later in the season he was largely responsible for his club's success as winners of the Champion Bat Tournament. This trophy, in the shape of a suitably engraved shield, was established by the Municipality of Port Elizabeth for a cricket competition in the Cape Colony.

Apart from playing for England, Frank Hearne had the distinction of being included four times in South African sides against his old country, the most notable occasion being the Test Match at Cape Town in March 1892 when Frank found himself facing his brothers George and Alec and his cousin John Thomas Hearne. The game was won easily by England, for the South African batting was weak, 13 of their wickets being taken by J.J. Ferris who had previously played for Australia. Another interesting feature of this match was the fact that the England batting was not much better than that of their opponents until Harry Wood, a Surrey man batting No. 8, scored 134 runs (his only century in first-class cricket). Together with J.T. Hearne, who made 40, the pair added 71 for the ninth wicket, which has stood as an England record in the series ever since. Apparently *Wisden*, along with the cricket authorities of the time, did not initially regard the game as a Test Match and so gave no details of the South African innings.

In 1892 Frank Hearne again distinguished himself for Western Province, this time in the third Currie Cup Tournament. Originally, the Cup had been presented by Sir Donald Currie to the best South African side against Major Warton's team during their visit in 1888/9, which turned out to be Kimberley. In 1891, C.A. Smith, who had captained Major Warton's team and remained in South Africa, considered that Transvaal could reasonably challenge Kimberley for the trophy, but in front of a record gate they failed by 58 runs in what became the second Currie Cup Tournament. The Third Tournament, embracing Transvaal, Griqualand West and Western Province, saw the Province victorious thanks to Frank's 102 in the first innings against Transvaal and 96 versus Griqualand West. Needless to say, he topped the batting with an average of 54.25.

The fourth Currie Cup Tournament took place at Cape Town in 1894, with players seeking to prove they were worthy of a place in South Africa's first cricket tour to England. In the event Western Province retained the trophy after vanquishing Natal in the final match by an innings and 60 runs, thanks to some solid batting for a total of 338, Frank Hearne scoring 25.

Frank, by now well over 30 years of age, was included in the inexperienced South African team chosen for the 1894 tour of England. Unluckily for them, it proved to be a very wet English summer, and this, together with poor attendance at the few first-class fixtures, all added up to a large financial failure.

It cannot be said that Frank enjoyed a great deal of success; his batting average in all matches was only 15.89 and his solitary wicket cost 56 runs. In the first match, against Lord Sheffield's XI at Brighton, Frank opened the South African innings and made a pair, followed by another duck against

Hampshire a few days later. His batting was disappointing, mostly low scores and a number of noughts, one of which was against Lord Cantelupe's XI at Bexhill on 13 and 14 August when he was caught and bowled by his brother Alec! His one really good performance was in the tenth match of the tour when the South Africans played Gloucestershire at Bristol . Frank made 56 in the first innings, out of a total of 185, and 104 in the second knock. The South African opener E.A. Halliwell also scored a century, 110, but nobody else reached double figures. The home county won by 5 wickets, mainly due to W.G. Grace's 129 not out in the first innings.

The next season, 1895/6, Frank played in all three Test Matches against Lord Hawke's touring team and although he was twice top scorer he did not hit more than 30 in any of his six Test Match innings, which gives some indication of the weak opposition faced by the English side.

From then on Frank did not play much cricket, occupying himself more and more with coaching and umpiring; in the latter capacity he appeared in six Test Matches from 1889-1906. He was the only ex-South African Test Match player to umpire in a Test until the advent of Bill Wade in 1969-70.

After he retired as an active player and accompanied South Africa to England as their umpire in 1905-6, he retained his interest in cricket whilst living at 18 Strubens Road, Mowbray, until his death at Groote Schuur Hospital, Capetown, on 14th July 1949, having watched the Test between South Africa and England a few weeks earlier. His wife, Rosa, had died on 24th March 1942.

Frank's eldest son, Frank Victor Alfonso Hearne, was a good cricketer who did not become a first-class player in spite of his ability. He was a very powerfully built man who, according to his son Raymond, did not believe in running too many singles if he could let the ball do the work. For instance, the victorious South African team which toured England in 1935 contained an extremely successful spin bowler, Xenophon Balaskas. Playing against the Fish Hoek Cricket Club soon after his return, Balaskas was working his way rapidly through the local batsmen until F.A.V. Hearne arrived at the crease and promptly lifted four or five consecutive balls from the worthy bowler out of the ground in no uncertain fashion.

George Alfred Lawrence (G.A.L.), Frank and Rosa's second son, did follow in his father's footsteps as a professional South African cricketer and his career is recounted in a separate chapter.

During his cricket career Frank was awarded numerous trophies and mementos in commemoration of outstanding performances, some of which are shown in the illustration on page 75. The silver cup held by one of his grandsons, Lionel Frank Hearne, was presented to him in 1889 at Kimberley for the best score versus 22 South Africans. The certificate is the Ally Sloper award.

Lest it be thought that Lionel is basking in the reflected glory of his grandfather, it must be mentioned that the redoubtable Sgt. Major himself was no mean sportsman; for instance, in a cricket match at Simonstown in 1931, playing for Gordons v. Dockyard, he hit 99 in forty minutes including 5 sixes and 14 fours. He played cricket for 41 years until he was 56 and was an opening bat for 25 years. He also played football and badminton, winning the Northern Transvaal League singles when he was 46, dropping only one set in the tournament. In his younger days he found time to play hockey on roller skates and squash, and was in fact another Hearne all-rounder like his younger brother Raymond George who played cricket, soccer, badminton and hockey on roller skates. Ray was another crack shot in the family, this time at pistol shooting.

Lionel was an excellent artist and, as is the case with several of his relatives, he has passed this talent on to his two daughters.

Frank loved his family dearly and mourned the death of an infant son Alexander Louis. His one big disappointment must have been the failure of his third son, Alex Edward Vivian Hearne, born on 29th (or 20th) September 1901, to live up to the expectations that were held of him. Alex was an excellent sportsman who did very well in his earlier years both as a player and an accountant, and could play the piano with the best, but his charm and good looks together with a penchant for party life led to a lack of ability to secure permanent employment.

Frank had inherited some of his father's sense of humour, and loved to recount an amusing event which had taken place when he played in Lord Sheffield's side against Shrewsbury's team which had toured Australia. He opened the innings with the great W.G. Grace, and the sight of the diminutive figure and his giant companion so tickled one spectator that he shouted "Look out, Frankie, mind he doesn't tread on you". Frank avoided his massive partner and scored 60 to the Doctor's 30. On another occasion, also involving W.G., Frank drove a ball from the Doctor for 6, which did not please the great man who told his fielder on the boundary "You could have caught it in your mouth".

Frank Hearne and his wife are remembered affectionately by their grandchildren, particularly Winston Hearne, a distant cousin of the author, who established a large and thriving fruit farm at Kiepersol in East Transvaal. It is extraordinary how the main features of Frank's character encompass those of his family at large. The artistic talent seems to run an erratic course through-out the Hearnes and is still evident in several of Frank's surviving relatives. It is fitting that Winston who, together with his cousin Raymond Hearne, is also a skilled and prolific painter, should conclude their grandfather's story.

"It was always a great treat for us younger members of the family to visit Grandad Frank and Granny Rosa where a huge spread would be laid out in a typical English-style dining room.

"They were truly gentle people, yet nobody pushed Grandpa around, he was always a perfect gentleman right to his last day, always happy to do good for others. Supported in all his activities by Granny he turned his hand to everything. His special interests were not unnaturally sports goods, especially cricket equipment, his garden and his collection of butterflies and insects; he was also an excellent painter in oils and watercolours. Both grandparents were accomplished musicians, playing the piano, violin and flute. Grandpa was a polished man, always neatly dressed, with a ready friendly smile for everyone. Even though he had sciatica in both hips and could only get about with the aid of two walking sticks, he was always ready to undertake tasks which a lesser mortal would have never considered possible!"

Chapter 8

Alec Hearne
(Kent 1884-1906)

ALEC, born on 22nd July 1863, was the youngest of the three brothers who played for Kent County Cricket Club. A fourth brother, Randolph, did not play first class cricket but merits his own chapter later on.

Like his brother Frank, Alec was a small and lightly-built young man, but this proved to be no drawback to his ability as a cricketer and although he began his career as a slow bowler it was always his ambition to become a competent batsman. Initially Alec was a leg-break bowler, slightly above normal pace, and it was this feature that was to prove such a success against the Australians, some of whom were completely baffled by this type of bowling. At that time Alec did not practise off-break bowling very often as he was only able to bowl so slowly that he did not get many wickets. However, after a bad strain he began to bowl off-breaks more frequently and on sticky wickets found that delivery to be his most effective. In his early days he batted at number 10, but improved until for years he opened the innings whilst remaining a stock bowler.

The earliest record of Alec playing cricket is in 1876, when at the age of thirteen he took seven wickets, four with consecutive balls, for three runs whilst playing for the Victoria Club versus Sydenham Comet. In 1879 and 1880 he usually played for the Mid-Kent Club and continued his remarkable bowling performances with averages of 3.15 and 4.11 in these two years. Among his outstanding efforts was nine wickets for nine runs for Mid-Kent versus Woolwich Ordnance Stores, the tenth man being run out! Other feats with the bat included 112 against the Royal School of Mines and 83 versus MCC and Ground.

In common with many other cricketers of the time, Alec Hearne played for a number of different clubs. He turned out several times for Blackheath Morden at the age of nineteen. Later on that same summer he really showed his capability as a batsman; when playing for Mr. Silverthorn's XI at Catford Bridge he made 39 out of his side's total of 78, and then just to show he could also bowl he took six of the Greville wickets. It is interesting to note that a

Five first-class Hearnes in 1905.

T.B. Hearne was also playing for Blackheath Morden at this time, but so far it has not been possible to prove that he was in any way part of the family.

It is fortunate that so many of Alec's early efforts appear on record and one can easily imagine the excited discussions that must have taken place at home when all the boys returned after a day's cricket to recount their various achievements to their father, who had become very proud of his sons' performances at such a young age; but even Old George in his wildest dreams could not have imagined just how much success lay ahead.

Alec's early success as an all-round cricketer secured him employment by the Private Banks Cricket Club in 1882 and 1883. Between 1884 and 1887 he played for the Mote Park Club at Maidstone. In his first year with the Mote he turned in some superb bowling feats:- 6 for 20 against Town Malling, 10 for 44 against Devonshire Park, Eastbourne, and he demolished MCC and Ground with 5 for 27 in the first innings and 6 for 14 in his opponents' second effort.

He appeared for the Kent CCC Second Eleven in the summer of 1884, shining mainly as a bowler when he took 6 of the Tonbridge and District wickets for 33 runs, and in a match against Gravesend he shattered their first innings by taking 8 of the 10 wickets for 59 runs.

By 1884, when he was 21 years old, Alec had played a few times for the Kent First Eleven when the then captain Philip Hilton suggested to Lord Harris that the young man should be included in the match against the Australians at Canterbury on 4th, 5th and 6th August. At first Lord Harris did not think that Alec was sufficiently strong or old enough to bear the strain of such an important match; however, despite being heavily criticised for doing so, he included Alec in the team, and the young man surprised everybody by taking a total of 7 wickets for 66 in the match, 5 in the first innings and 2 in the second, which was a major contribution to the only defeat suffered by the Australians that year against the counties. The other reason for Kent's victory was the fine batting of Lord Harris and Frank Hearne in their second innings.

In the last week of August Alec, playing with his two brothers and cousin Herbert in the Kent side, had a total of 8 for 77 against Somerset at Tunbridge Wells. *Wisden* affectionately but erroneously refers to ". . . young Alexander Hearne . . ." (his birth certificate clearly shows he was christened Alec).

He had a fine season with the ball in 1885, playing in 13 County matches and taking 64 wickets at an average 14.32 apiece. His best efforts were at Sheffield in May when he captured a total of 13 Yorkshire wickets at a cost of 48 runs in 56 overs and at Tonbridge in August when he had 5 Hampshire wickets for 15 runs in their first innings.

KENT v THE AUSTRALIANS
at Canterbury on 4, 5 and 6 August 1884
Kent won by 96 runs

KENT

First Innings		Second Innings	
F.A. MacKinnon Esq c Palmer b Spofforth	28	b Palmer	29
F. Hearne b Palmer b Spofforth	7	c Bannerman b Boyle	45
G.G. Hearne b Palmer	27	b Spofforth	6
Lord Harris b Spofforth	2	b Palmer	60
W.H. Patterson Esq b Giffen	19	c Spofforth b Palmer	3
C. Wilson Esq b Giffen	37	b Palmer	3
M.C. Kemp not out	11	b Palmer	21
S. Christopherson Esq b Palmer	1	c Bonnor b Midwinter	14
J. Wootton b Palmer	0	b Palmer	8
A. Hearne c Bonnor b Giffen	5	b Palmer	2
F. Lipscomb Esq b Palmer	4	not out	0
Extras	28	Extras	22
	169		**213**

THE AUSTRALIANS

First Innings		First Innings	
P.S. McDonnell c F. Hearne b A. Hearne	80	b Lipscomb	19
G.J. Bonnor b Wootton	5	c Patterson b A. Hearne	9
W. Murdoch c Harris b Wootton	24	c Harris b A. Hearne	4
G.Giffen c C.G. Hearne b Wootton	5	c Kemp b Lipscomb	0
A.C.Bannerman run out	18	not out	35
H.J.H. Scott c Harris b A. Hearne	19	c Harris b Christopherson	22
W. Midwinter b Wootton	12	b Wootton	8
J.McC. Blackham st Kemp b A. Hearne	6	b Wootton	0
G.E.Palmer c F.Hearne b A.Hearne	0	b Christopherson	2
F.R.Spofforth c Kemp b A.Hearne	0	c & b Christopherson	4
H.F. Boyle not out	4	b Wootton	0
Extras	4	Extras	6
	177		**109**

Australian Bowling

	Overs	Mdns.	Runs	Wkts.		Overs	Mdns.	Runs	Wkts.
Spofforth	39	23	45	3	......	16	3	39	1
Midwinter	12	3	28	–	......	14	7	13	1
Palmer	38.3	20	52	4	......	36.2	14	74	7
Giffen	12	6	16	3	......	18	6	43	–
Boyle						10	3	22	1

Kent Bowling

	Overs	Mdns.	Runs	Wkts.	Overs	Mdns.	Runs	Wkts.
Mr. Lipscomb	16	1	41	–	13	2	40	2
Wootton	36	12	72	4	22.3	13	21	3
Mr. Christopherson	14	4	24	–	19	15	12	3
Hearne, A.	21.1	10	36	5	16	9	30	2

A fine performance of 8 for 30 for MCC against Yorkshire at Lord's in May was the highlight of Alec's 1888 season. The County was strengthened usefully by the emergence of his cousin Walter, a younger brother of Herbert. One highlight in an otherwise rather dismal year for Alec was a score of 128 for the Mote v. Sherncliffe Camp when he helped F.M. Atkins (364) to add 492 runs! Another unusual occasion occurred in June when Kent played Lancashire at Gravesend, and the four Hearnes batted 1, 2, 3 and 4 for the host County.

Alec bowled with more success for Kent in 1888 when he finished second in the County averages with 41 wickets in ten matches at a cost of 10.40 each. *Wisden* remarks that in this season Kent had in one sense too many bowlers of a kind in Martin, Walter Wright and Wootton, who were all left-handers, and with G.G. Hearne who was still a good change bowler but of the same character.

By 1889 Alec Hearne, apart from his main role as a bowler, was also becoming an established batsman for his County, opening the innings and making significant contributions to Kent's successes. The County side, however, was to be weakened by the loss of Frank Hearne and of Lord Harris who played his last game for some time at the end of the season as he had been appointed Governor of Bombay, sailing for India in March 1890. For most of this year, Alec's performances for his County were very disappointing, particularly at a time when Kent were unable to field a team that was either strong or consistent. Had they always been able to select the eleven that turned out during and after Canterbury week they would have been able to challenge the strongest sides. The improvement in his team's performance co-incided with an upturn in Alec's fortunes, and he finished the season in great form, scoring 72 against Surrey at Canterbury and 23 and 59 versus Yorkshire at Maidstone. He also took 5 for 20 in Yorkshire's first innings, following this with 7 for 56 against Surrey at the Oval, his achievement on this occasion including 11 maidens in his 33 overs. The Australians were again beaten by Kent on 4th, 5th and 6th August 1890 at Canterbury, when the County won by 108 runs. Kent scored 145 and 205, Alec making 24 and 35, to which the Australians could only reply with 114 and 128.

In 1891 the Kent attack rested almost wholly on the dependable shoulders of their three regular bowlers, F. Martin, A. Hearne and W. Wright, who took 98, 40 and 56 wickets respectively in the County's first class matches. These figures would have been greatly improved but for dreadful fielding and numerous dropped catches. Alec made 390 runs for the County at an average of 17.16, but brother George could only manage an average of 9.8 and in some quarters it was not understood why he was not put on to bowl more often in view of his batting failures.

In 1891/92 Alec was included in W.W. Read's team which went to South Africa, and he was in the side which played the only Test Match of the tour. Alec played well in the first three matches of the tour, scoring 61 and 91 against XV of Cape Colony in the second match. In fact, he had a successful tour with both the bat and the ball, and after the first two or three matches he soon got used to the matting wickets. He found he could make the ball do a little more than he could on England's fast wickets, but he also discovered that the ball did not leave the pitch quite as fast, and that a good length ball seldom got up above the top of the stumps. He considered that his brother Frank, who batted against them two or three times, had not lost any of his skills and played some good innings against them. Alec got Frank caught off his bowling on one occasion but Frank soon got his own back in another match by bowling Alec when he had made a very good score. One thing that surprised Alec was the fact that although the heat was very great it was not as trying to field during a long innings as it would have been on a very hot day in England.

As Alec's *Wisden* obituary states:- "He accomplished several fine feats in games with various Australian teams". Indeed he did, for in addition to the 1884 and 1894 victories he also took part in the 1893 match when the Australians lost on the St. Lawrence ground. Alec made 20 and 39 and took 8 wickets. In the same year he averaged 38 against the Australians, with a highest score of 120 for the South at the Oval, and obtained 17 wickets for 12 runs apiece. He played another three-figure innings against the Australians in 1899, getting 168 for W.G. Grace's XI at the Crystal Palace.

As we have noted, Alec was credited with a Test Match appearance during the 1891/92 tour of South Africa. This was the unusual match when Alec and his brother G.G., together with their cousin J.T. Hearne, opposed their brother Frank who was playing for South Africa.

On 10th May 1892 Alec Hearne married Elizabeth Rose Eve at the Wesleyan Chapel, Tunbridge Road, Maidstone. He was 28 years old and his bride aged 22. Alec's address was given as Catford Bridge, Lewisham, and Elizabeth, whose father George was a papermaker, lived at 1 Church Street, Tovil, Maidstone. They had four children, Gladys, Phyllis, who married Frank Merchant, but not the Kent cricketer of those days, Doris and Eustace. They were a popular couple with many friends including close acquaintances in Scotland; in fact photographs exist showing Alec wearing full Scottish dress including a kilt! Alec celebrated the year of his marriage by scoring his first century for Kent, carrying his bat for 116 versus Gloucestershire at Canterbury on 1st, 2nd and 3rd August. In acknowledgement of this performance a collection of £50 was made on his behalf.

Although Alec still opened the batting for Kent in 1893 and played a few excellent innings for them, his average of 19.26 was not nearly as good as that of the previous summer when his figures were 32.18. He made 22 and 43 not out for the Players against the Gentlemen at the Oval on 6th, 7th and 8th July, but did not take any wickets and was not selected to play in the corresponding match at Lord's.

The following season, 1894, was rather a poor one for Alec with the bat; he played a few very good innings but was nowhere near his best form. Against Middlesex at Tonbridge, his cousin John Thomas Hearne bowled him out in both innings for 1 and 85. In spite of J.T. taking 6 for 77 and 4 for 87, Kent won the match.

Alec's bowling was much more successful and together with Wright he gave strong support to Martin and his cousin Walter Hearne, who were both at their best on the wet summer's soft wickets. Among his feats that summer were 5 maiden overs with 4 wickets for no runs in the Somerset match at Taunton, and 5 wickets for 7 runs against the South Africans at Bexhill whilst playing for Viscount Cantelupe's Eleven.

Although no details or precise dates are available, M.W. Luckin in his *History of South African Cricket* states that Alec had a coaching engagement in Durban. Other professional English cricketers engaged by the club were Cox of Sussex and an unspecified Gunn from Nottinghamshire.

If Alec did spend the winter of 1894/5 in the sunny climate of Natal then it certainly did him good, for he enjoyed an outstanding season for Kent the following summer, heading the county's batting and bowling figures. He averaged over 28 with the bat compared to 15 the previous season, and took 66 wickets as against 40 in 1894.

He shared five three-figure opening partnerships with J.R. Mason at a time when they could be considered among the best opening pairs in the country. One of his most memorable performances was against Gloucestershire at Gravesend in May when he scored 155 out of a Kent first innings total of 470. Gloucestershire made 443 in reply (W.G. Grace 257), Alec collecting 4 of their wickets for 93. Kent could only manage a miserable 76 in their second knock, Alec making 22 not out. Gloucestershire won easily and Alec took the only wicket to fall in the second innings, while W.G., who scored 73 not out, was on the field for every ball of the match.

Another match of note was against Oxford University at Maidstone on 27th, 28th and 29th June, when Alec made 105 in Kent's first innings, putting

A young Alec.

Alec taking guard at the Oval.

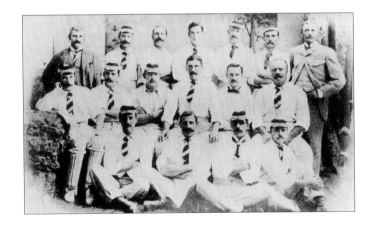

Second English team in South Africa 1891-2.
(l to r from back row)
J.Leaney (umpire), E.Leaney, F.Martin, G.W.Ayres, A.D.Pougher,
W.Chatterton, Edwin Ash (Manager)
H.Wood, G.G.Hearne, J.T.Hearne, W.W.Read, J.J.Ferris, W.L.Murdoch.
W.Brockwell, G.Brann, V.Barton, A.Hearne.

F.H.Huish and Alec Hearne.

on 134 for the first wicket with Mason (50) and was then out for a 'duck' in his second effort. Pelham Warner, who was in the victorious Oxford side which won by 215 runs, scored 2 and 76.

There was an extraordinary match at the Catford Bridge Ground versus Surrey on 22nd and 23rd July; Kent were dismissed for 43 in the first innings and after Alec and Mason opened with 118 in their second innings, no other batsman scored more than 8! The explanation was, of course, a dreadful wicket and Alec took full advantage of the treacherous conditions suffered by the hapless batsmen, taking 8 for 72 in the first innings of Surrey who won by 10 wickets. This was followed by another great piece of bowling a week later when Kent played Somerset at Blackheath; Alec scored 32 and 51 and took 7 for 29 (21 overs, 11 maidens), and 3 for 37.

This year of 1895 proved to be Alec Hearne's best season as a first class batsman. He made a total of 1,477 runs, reaching a thousand in July, but even his great all-round abilities could not save Kent from suffering one of their very worst seasons.

Alec could not match his superb form of 1895 during the following season. Nevertheless, his first class matches yielded a batting average of over 21 and he took a total of 73 wickets at an average of 28, with 63 wickets for less than 17 each for Kent. This was the year that the Kent club was able to buy the St. Lawrence Ground and from then onwards was able to improve facilities for both players and spectators at this attractive centre of Kent cricket.

1897 was to prove another disappointing summer's cricket for Alec, who was badly affected by a severe strain which meant that he could not achieve anything like his fine form of the previous season. There is no doubt that his inability to maintain his high standard of play formed one of the main reasons for Kent's poor showing; also, they did not have a bowler to fill Walter Hearne's place which underlines how dependent they were on the all-round play of their best professional.

Having dwelt on Kent's woeful performance in 1897 it is pleasant to be able to record that the season of 1898 represented a great improvement, although *Wisden* reported that "It cannot be said that any of the (Kent) bowling presented real difficulties to first rate batsmen on good wickets". One is inclined to reply that first rate batsmen on good wickets are rarely troubled by other than exceptional bowling. It is no surprise to learn that Alec Hearne and J.R. Mason formed the backbone of the team throughout the season. Before the end of June Alec scored three centuries for his County, 117 *v* Sussex at Catford Bridge on 9th, 10th and 11th June, 112 *v* Somerset at Tonbridge on 2nd, 3rd and 4th June when with W.H. Patterson (111) he put on 220 for the second wicket and 117 *v* Warwickshire also at Tonbridge on 20th, 21st and 22nd June. Later in the summer during the benefit match which brought him £615 19s 6d at Canterbury on 1st, 2nd and 3rd August, he scored 80 not out and 74 against Lancashire, and 51 not out and 48 against Essex at Tonbridge three weeks later.

In 1899 Kent distinguished themselves by beating the Australians again at Canterbury. The tourists had built up a first innings lead of 43, scoring 227 to Kent's 184. The Australians were then dismissed for 94, and Kent were thus faced with having to score 138 runs to win in the last innings. At one stage they looked like losing, having lost 8 wickets for 114, but in an exciting finish H.C. Stewart and G. Weigall saw them home, Alec having made 20 and 17.

Although he often played extremely well this year, Alec could not match his county batting and bowling of 1898, but he did achieve a total of 910 runs and took 53 wickets. His best efforts included 162 not out against Nottingham at Trent Bridge when he and Mason (181 not out) made one of their most famous stands, in this case 351, which was then a third wicket record for Kent and was not bettered for 35 years.

By 1900 Alec had reached the age of thirty-seven and the prospect of retirement within the next few years must have been in his mind. Kent still badly needed his services, along with those of the only other capped professional Huish, particularly as two of their long-serving bowlers, Martin and Wright, had retired, and the County's prospects looked bleak. In this year Alec did not enjoy a particularly good season, but he was still able to make some important all-round contributions to what turned out to be a surprisingly successful summer for Kent, who finished joint third with Sussex. His best feats were with the ball, taking 5 for 50 against Yorkshire at Catford on 10th, 11th and 12th May, 5 for 44 versus Essex at Maidstone later on in May, and against Sussex at Tonbridge he scored 46 and took 5 for 68. At Clifton in August he did the hat trick in the first innings against Gloucestershire, his victims being F.H.B. Champain, G.L. Jessop and A.G. Richardson; strangely, he took no more wickets in the innings.

Kent, finishing joint seventh with Hampshire in the County table, enjoyed a fairly successful season in 1901, during which Alec Hearne continued to render valuable services for his county. Without being particularly consistent with the bat he scored 972 runs at an average of just under 30, helped in no small degree by one long and patient innings of five hours for 152 not out against Essex at Leyton late in May. He took 48 wickets for the county at a cost of 24.64 for each wicket.

Perhaps it was due to his advancing years as a professional that the slow wickets of 1902 were not to his liking, for he did not often achieve anything like his best. Nevertheless, he took 7 Somerset wickets for 34 runs at Maidstone in July. In August he scored 73 at Canterbury against Surrey and later on in the same month, at Catford, he took 5 Yorkshire wickets for 22 runs. Another good piece of bowling that year was 4 for 10 versus Gloucestershire at Tonbridge.

Alec Hearne commenced the season of 1903 so out of form that he was dropped from the team for one match. This event was so unusual that it merited a mention in *Wisden*, which gives an indication of the kind of service normally given to his county by this worthy professional player. This was a season when Kent had many bad results, in spite of the outstanding bowling of Colin Blythe. At the Oval, Blythe (12-67) and Alec (7-66) bowled unchanged throughout both the Surrey innings.

At the end of that season Alec was to enjoy one other overseas tour, as Kent had been approached by the Philadelphian cricket team, which had had a successful tour of England that year, with a view to inviting the Kent County XI to visit them in September at the end of the season, under the auspices of the Associated Clubs of Philadelphia. Initially it seemed unlikely that Kent would get a sufficiently strong side together to do themselves justice, as at that time cricket had a very strong following in America where several of the clubs could be counted upon to give them a good run for their money. The amateurs on their own could not form a strong enough team. One or two of the professionals who were approached made a very generous gesture when they offered to go in return for their expenses and a ten-pound note; this offer was naturally accepted with alacrity by the remainder of the squad. The professionals involved were Alec Hearne, Huish, Blythe and Seymour.

The team left early in September on the White Star liner *Oceanic*, their destination being New York. They had rather a rough journey, with a hurricane on the day they landed, but apparently the weather was not quite as bad as the New York press made it out to be. They passed swiftly through Customs and started off at once from Jersey City to Philadelphia, where they arrived that evening. In his account of the tour C.J. Burnup did not express a high opinion of their hotel, the Aldine in Chestnut Street. At that time relations between England and Ireland were very strained and as most of the waiters were Irish, it appears that the Englishmen were not viewed with favour. On 18th and 19th September, Kent played 18 Colts of Philadelphia at the Manheim Ground, Germantown, one of the best in America, and they won quite easily. They dismissed the Colts in the first innings for 79 and in the second innings for 114, when Alec struck his length and took 8 wickets for 25 runs. Burnup was particularly impressed by his opponents' fielding, and felt that the Americans featured so well in this aspect of the game because of the high standard of ball play by their baseball players.

At that time the Manheim Ground boasted a superb Club House with facilities such as overnight accommodation, various recreation rooms, a skittle alley and a fine swimming pool in which, Burnup relates, mixed bathing was permitted, the whole enterprise being run more as a social club than a cricket club. On one day's play a leading member provided the visitors with such an excellent lunch that when they dropped some catches during the afternoon he remarked that he felt he had done his share for America!

After successful matches against Philadelphia and New York on the Livingstone Ground at Staten Island, the Kent team visited Atlantic City and Niagara, sailing from New York, after touring the city, in the *S.S. Cedric*, arriving home on 17th October.

Kent fielded a rapidly improving eleven in 1904; in fact, there was so much talent available that Alec and K.L. Hutchings were not included in the team during Canterbury week. Alec was soon back in the side and justified his inclusion with 100 not out against Middlesex at Lord's. He was sixth in the Kent averages this year, scoring 723 runs in his seventeen matches at an average of 28.92 and taking 21 wickets for 19.42 runs each. Kent were third in the County table.

Next year Kent again won 10 County games but, losing seven matches as against four in 1904, they dropped back to sixth place. This decline was probably due to the fact that the bowlers fell away badly. Alec was second in his County's bowling averages, having 32 wickets for 22.15 each, but his batting declined to 20.46.

1906 saw the retirement of Alec Hearne as a County cricketer, but it proved a very memorable year in several respects, for Kent won the County Championship literally at the post with a side reckoned to be the outstanding example of county cricket during the 'Golden Age' of the game. They had so much talent available that even Frank Woolley, who was rapidly becoming such a great all-rounder, was not an automatic choice. Alec performed at his very best in the match at Worcester when he made 154 not out, this at the age of 43, batting all one day and part of the next.

At the end of the season and of his playing career, Alec Hearne had scored 13,897 runs at an average of 21.85 and taken 1,036 wickets at an average of 19.82, more runs and wickets than any other Kent cricketer up to that time. Four times he made over 1,000 runs, and he batted throughout his side's innings on six occasions. In 1893 he was among *Wisden's* Five Cricketers of the Year.

During his long career Alec undertook numerous coaching engagements, an activity which he continued for some years after his retirement. One such appointment involved another visit to South Africa in 1910/11 when he predicted a great future for a youngster named Fairless Nicholson. J.W.F. Nicholson eventually played three times for South Africa in 1927/8 (highest score 78) and for Natal between 1923 and 1930 (highest score 252 not out). He appeared for Oxford University in 1923 but failed to get his Blue. He emigrated as a teacher to Ireland and died there in 1935, aged 35.

The decision to dispense with Alec's services as a County player was considered by many to be questionable at the time, but eventually it was thought best to adhere to the policy of bringing on young players. The decision was accepted by Alec in his usual philosophical manner for, after all, he had had a benefit match against Lancashire in 1898 and MCC made him a similar award of the Middlesex *v* Hampshire match at Lord's in 1913.

After his retirement as a County player Alec coached at the Kent Nursery in Tonbridge for several years. Whilst he was also coaching at King's School, Canterbury, in 1925 his cousin Walter Hearne died so he took over the job of County scorer in 1926. G.J.V. Weigall then assisted with the coaching at Tonbridge. Although he was severely handicapped with rheumatism towards the end of this appointment, Alec continued as scorer until 1939.

A quiet man who became even more taciturn in his later years, he resembled so many of his cricketing family with their self-effacing manner and rare moments of dry humour which occurred on unexpected occasions. For some years he lived with his daughter Phyllis at 93 Hayes Road, Bromley. Alec Hearne eventually died at 12 Westgate Road, Beckenham, on 16th May 1952, aged 88 years.

Chapter 9

Randolph Hearne

RANDOLPH, the youngest of George Hearne's children, was born in 1870 at Southgate. He was overshadowed by his three famous elder brothers and information on Randolph's life is scanty, although it is known that he was a keen cricketer. In addition to his regular appearance in the family team against Ealing Dean he was a member of the Panther Cricket Club, which was composed of the employees of John Taylor and Sons of Queen Street Place. There are several records of his appearances for this club between 1892 and 1895 when they played in the Catford-Dulwich area. His best score was in July 1892 when he opened the Panther innings with 74 against Granville (Lee) at Lee. He also appeared for St. John's Wood Ramblers.

On 13th October 1896 Randolph married Blanche Gregory at the Parish Church of Cheltenham and the marriage certificate gives his occupation as "gymnast". This might indicate that he was a sportsmaster at a local school or college, but there is no supporting evidence.

No further details of Randolph's life would have been forthcoming but for the fact that his wife lived to celebrate her 100th birthday on Wednesday 12th January 1972, and in a newspaper article reporting an interview with her the old lady recalled that soon after their marriage Randolph had been offered a job by Lord Eglinton on his estate in Scotland, as a consequence of which they moved to Ayrshire.

This could have made further research more difficult, but fortunately Arthur Brack, the well-known genealogist, an enthusiastic cricketer himself, had been acquainted with several old professionals who had played for the Eglinton team. It was he who suggested that a perusal of old numbers of the *Irvine Herald* at the Newspaper Library at Colindale might prove fruitful. This indeed proved to be the case, and a copy of that newspaper dated 7th May 1897 contains the following account:-

CRICKET

IRVINE v. LORD EGLINTON'S XI

The cricket season opened at Eglinton on Saturday, when his lordship led his men against the Irvine. The pitch was in capital condition. For the first match of the season the scoring was surprising, and we hope the form will be kept up. Lord Eglinton's team batted first, and in about two hours the score had reached 200, shortly after which the closure was applied, the score standing at 211 for five wickets. Capt. Cunningham was highest scorer with 77, which included thirteen 4's. Lord Montgomerie, who showed great improvement in his style, came next with 58, which included ten 4's. Hearne came next with 42, and Lord Eglinton next with a well got 32. E.D. Prothero, Major Aikman, and T.C. Barbour, all playing a good game for their respective scores. The Irvine team was easily disposed of for 39, none of the players showing anything like their usual form. The bowling honours were evenly divided. Scores:-

LORD EGLINTON'S XI

Hearne (prof.), c Burns b McPetrie,	42
E.D. Prothero, c Jeffrey b Mitchell,	11
Capt. Cunningham, b Burns,	77
Major Aikman, c Jeffrey b McPetrie,	17
Ld. Eglinton, c Kyle b Mitchell,	32
Ld. Montgomerie, not out,	58
T.C. Barbour, not out,	6
T.C. Mathieson,	
Hon. W. Montgomerie, } to bat	
A. Cunningham	
D. Stevenson,	
Extras,	1
Total (for five wickets)	211

In answer Irvine were all out for a miserable 3 runs.

Other accounts of the Eglinton Castle matches appeared throughout that summer and the preceding season with references to ". . . Hearne, the professional . . .", no doubt to distinguish him from the more illustrious members of the team! Further information regarding the location of the cricket ground and of Eglinton Castle was generously provided by the Troon and District Family History Society.

Shortly afterwards the present Earl of Eglinton and Winton kindly supplied an extract from an account of the nineteenth century family history written by his grandfather as follows:-

Extract from a hand written book of 'Family Reminiscences' by my grandfather, the 16th Earl of Eglinton (1880 - 1945). 'He' refers to my greatgrandfather who was the keen cricketer and who lived from 1848 - 1919.

"He started quite humbly by playing against the local teams and his team would consist of such of the family as was available – Longmuir – the groundsman – a very subtle bowler – G's 2nd horseman – Jimmy Finnie – a fast bowler – Boyd Cunningham – a really good first-class cricketer – Graham Findley – wicketkeeper – a Glasgow business man – Col. Roberts Aikman of the Ross – Hamilton – a fair cricketer and so on but the class improved rapidly and a Pro appeared on the scene who was groundsman as well – a young Hearne of the famous family was the first Pro, a very nice man, not a great cricketer, but quite good enough at that time. Then followed A.E. Street, Welford, Gregson and Minto, while other Pros were got up from England for special matches. Street was the best permanent Pro and stayed many years. He could bowl exceedingly well at times and at other times exceedingly badly. Mr. Paterson, the Head Carpenter, or to give him his proper title 'Clerk of the Works', was Secretary and also got up a booklet at the end of each season giving an account of the matches, batting and bowling averages, and so now the racquet court was used as a pavilion for luncheons and changing rooms upstairs for the visiting team, downstairs for the home side. A wooden and canvas pavilion was put up each session where the ladies looked on, gossiped and so on and was always called "The Hareem", while there were benches all round the boundary where anybody who liked could sit and look on and on a fine Saturday there would be quite a good crowd from Irvine and Kilwinning – now I have mentioned a few of the original players but the mainstay of the side was the already mentioned Boyd Cunningham – he was a nephew of Mother's and deserves special mention – he was a really good cricketer and if he had lived in England and played for a county I am sure he would have been asked to play for the Gentlemen. He was also just about the best man to hounds I ever saw and could play all games above a bit and was the straightest and nicest man you could want to meet".

There appears to be no record of when Randolph terminated his employment with Lord Eglinton but he did return to live for many years at Salperton, a tiny village in Gloucestershire a short distance north-west of Northleach. Here he may have continued his work as a groundsman on one of the large estates. An old inhabitant of the village, who had lived opposite Randolph and his wife, thought it rather sad that the couple had lived a lonely life with no children or visitors, and recalled that Randolph often spoke wistfully of his brothers. This may have been the case later on in his life when his older relatives might have found the journey to this remote location rather difficult. Certainly, Randolph was still in close touch with them up to the time of his marriage, at which at least two of his cousins from Ealing were present, Kate Maud Hearne and Lavinia Wakefield, daughters of 'Old Tom' Hearne.

Randolph died of pneumonia on 15 May 1955, aged 85 years. A copy of the death certificate shows his occupation to have been 'Professional Cricketer (Retired)'; in common with a number of his relatives, most of whom were very good players, he never achieved first-class status.

Randolph in later years.

Chapter 10

George Alfred Lawrence Hearne
(Western Province 1910/11-1926/7)

GEORGE ALFRED LAWRENCE HEARNE, born at 61 Blythe Vale, Catford, on 27th March 1888, the second of three sons of Frank and Rosa (née Howes), was only a very small child when his father, returning from the tour of South Africa with Major R.G. Warton's team in 1889, decided that the family should uproot and settle in Cape Town. (Many writers have stated that Frank remained in South Africa after the tour; this is not so, for he came back to England first).

G.A.L., or George as he has been known to all, soon became an excellent cricketer, his first big match being for Western Province when aged 16 and still at his school, Wynberg High, with his brothers Frank V.A. and Alex who played hockey for the Province. George also played hockey for South Africa and participated in tennis, swimming and all field games. His famous father Frank played for both England and South Africa, and George eventually provided the first instance in South African Test cricket of a son following in his father's footsteps.

George first played for Western Province in 1910-11, seven years after his father's final match, but he had little chance to establish himself before the First World War brought cricket to a halt for six years, after which he played until 1927. On 17th March 1917 George Hearne married Ruby Woodville Stevens at Kenilworth, Cape Province. Ruby, named after her mother Emma Ruby Strang, born on 10th August 1895 at Oudtshoorn, Cape Province, was an excellent tennis and bowls player. They had two sons, George Winston (usually known as Winston) who married Hazel Archer, and Neil Woodville who married Doreen Duffy. It was an ill trick of fate that Neil should die so soon after he began to assist with the history of his branch of the family, for he furnished many details which are contained in this account. Initially, Neil and Doreen lived at Pinelands. It was during these days in Cape Town that "Smokey", as he was known in cricket circles, became widely rated as the best wicket keeper in the Western Province and could well have taken up a career in first class cricket.

In 1919-20 G.A.L. batted with great assurance to score 41 and 55 for Western Province against the Australian Imperial Forces team as an opening batsman, and was selected for one of the two unofficial "Tests". The following season he played several sound innings to help Western Province win the Currie Cup, his best effort being 78 against Transvaal in a vital match which his side won on the first innings. Opening the bowling against Border, he collected 3 for 9 in ten overs to record the best figures of his career.

He was twelfth man for the final match of the series against Australia in 1921-22, being unlucky not to have played after making 78 (out of a total of 153) and 33 for Western Province against the tourists in the game immediately preceding the Test.

G.A.L. Hearne made history in the last match of the season when scoring 106 against Natal in Durban to provide the first instance of a son and father recording a century in Currie Cup cricket. In spite of this effort, Natal won the match, ensuring a three-way tie for the trophy between themselves, Transvaal and Western Province. George, with 432 runs at 43.20, finished second to Dave Nourse of Natal (444 runs) in the Currie Cup aggregates for the season and was by far the most successful Western Province batsman. He also bowled well to take eight wickets at 21.50, his best effort being 3 for 53 against Transvaal, which with his innings of 39 and 70 played a major rôle in his side's victory in a vital match.

Having moved into the country, G.A.L. represented South Western Districts in a non-first-class match against the MCC touring team in 1922-23, scoring 31 and 11. Somewhat surprisingly, he was chosen for the First Test, but fully justified his selection with two valuable innings of 28 and 27 as an opener in a match which South Africa won by 168 runs, their first Test victory since 1911. Failure in both innings in the second Test led to George being left out for the rest of the series. However, he did a fine job substituting for the injured South African wicketkeeper Tommy Ward in the first innings and held three catches.

This performance could have been a factor in his selection for the 1924 tour to England, which he made as deputy wicketkeeper to Ward. In all matches on that trip he scored 463 runs at 21.04 (413 at 21.73 in first-class games) and appeared in the final Test at the Oval, where he opened the innings and was unluckily run out for four. His best efforts were to top-score against United Services with 68 and a fighting 33 on a spiteful pitch against Lancashire in a match lost by an innings.

It was on this 1924 tour that play was halted during a match in which George was participating. He received a telegram whilst batting which he

G.A.L. Hearne in his "Springbok" cap at the Lords nursery.

G.A.L. (right) at his retirement presentation with Mr. Katral.

promptly stuffed in his pocket without reading the message, and took guard again. However, the opposing captain, probably intrigued to learn the contents, told him to go ahead and read it. It said, "Cushion arrived, tassel and all". After congratulations from the fieldsman and clapping from some of the crowd who had learned the news, the game continued. The wire in effect announced the birth of George's son Neil, and for these details the author is grateful to George's grandson, (Neil's son), who is a distant cousin in Pietermaritzburg and another J.W. Hearne.

G.A.L. Hearne's career ended in 1926-27, when he batted as well as ever to make his highest first-class score, 138 against Griqualand West at Newlands. In the next match he played superbly to make 34 in a total of 74 against Transvaal, no one else reaching double figures, and followed with 35 in the second innings. However, Western Province lost by an innings.

In his forty-one first-class appearances he made 1981 runs at 28.30, captured 14 wickets (28.64) and took 38 catches.

A talented and versatile cricketer, George lived to almost the same age as his father, being ninety years and two hundred and thirty-one days old when he died at Barberton, E. Transvaal, on 13th November 1978, just two days short of Frank Hearne's age at death. Like his father, he was the oldest ex-Springbok at the time of his death.

Both Neil and Winston, and their cousin Raymond, who so ably contributed to the family story after Neil's death, inherited their grandfather's skill as artists working mainly in oils.

An insight into G.A.L.'s character is provided by Winston Hearne, who writes: "He believed the umpire was there to govern the game and he hence never ever raised an eyebrow at the umpire's decision. He upheld fair play and was a bit fanatical on being a good sportsman.

"Like his parents, he was musical and was at his happiest when playing the piano. He was excellent at this instrument, as he was taught classical piano as a youngster, yet he was bashful to play to big audiences. Although he was of a reasonably quiet disposition, he loved to show us kids tricks, spinning the ball, card and money tricks, balancing finger feats. He had tremendous strength in his nimble fingers.

"He started his career with the Government Services as Surveyor of Excise, and during his time was moved from pillar to post, especially in his earlier years. This was when, while in Oudtshoorn, he met my mother Ruby. He was exceptionally conscientious at his work and was quick and accurate with figures. This, I think, was because his department was lenient and encouraging when it came to time off for sport.

"In his later years he took up bowls and became a top class competitor, playing League games until he had turned 87 years of age. After that, he sat back, watching and fussing the dogs he loved. He liked spotting the wild birds around his home. It was a pleasure seeing his eyes light up and sparkle when he watched cricket programmes on the T.V., yet immediately afterwards he couldn't tell you much other than that he had thoroughly enjoyed it.

"Like his father, Frank, my dad George was a gentleman in every respect, and everyone loved him dearly for that. He was always neat and tidy and liked things in their place. He respected everybody and always treated all courteously and never ever wanted to inconvenience anyone.

"The nurses, who were the last to care for him, praised his consideration towards the staff who finally saw him to the end".

Chapter 11

Herbert Hearne
(Kent 1884-1886)

HERBERT HEARNE, born at Chalfont St. Giles, Buckinghamshire on 15th March 1862, was the eldest brother of a trio who all became first class cricketers, the others being Walter, who like Herbert played for Kent, and John Thomas (J.T.) who played for Middlesex.

The boy's parents were William, a builder and undertaker like his father and grandfather and Mary (neé Montague). They had several other children, namely Henry who became a schoolmaster, Joseph who carried on the family business as a builder and undertaker, Annie who married George Budden, William another promising cricketer who did not achieve first class status, and Mary.

After he left school Herbert worked for the family business and became a proficient carpenter, a skill which was to serve him well in later years. He played local cricket from an early age; although it is not known for certain how he became engaged by Kent it seems reasonable to assume that old Uncle George and his sons, Frank and Alec had a great deal to do with it. The Hearnes were a closely knit family, well aware of their relations' good (and bad) points.

Although he was only a moderate batsman and average fieldsman his main ability was fast round-arm bowling, and it was for the latter activity that he was engaged by Kent for his short professional career between 1884 and 1886. Herbert's modest figures for the County were 252 runs in 27 completed innings (av. 9.33) and 57 wickets for 24.82 runs apiece. Probably his best performances were 5 for 84 against Yorkshire at Sheffield in 1884, 5 for 27 versus MCC at Lord's in 1885 including the wickets of A.N. Hornby and the arch stonewaller W.H. Scotton (clean bowled), and 5 for 60 and 2 for 43 against Hampshire at Southampton in the same year.

Unfortunately he was forced into early retirement, due to a knee injury, much to the disappointment of the Kent Club who felt that he could have developed into a valuable attacking opening bowler; he still managed to play some minor cricket and turned out for Buckinghamshire in 1891. There was no alternative but for him to return to the building trade and continue his work as a carpenter. It was whilst working at his old trade in London that he met and married Mary Ann Bendall, born in Cambridgeshire, daughter of Isaac Bendall, a fellow carpenter. The ceremony took place on 6th October 1886 at the Parish Church of All Saints, Haggerston E.8, their place of residence being given as No. 11 Lee Street and their ages as both 27 years old.

Soon after their marriage Herbert and his wife settled down at Chalfont St. Giles and raised a large family of eleven children, most of whom are seen on the photograph on page 108 together with their parents. Mary Ann still found time to line the coffins that her husband made. Tragically Herbert died in June 1906 at the age of forty-four after being in poor health for some considerable time. He was one of the tallest men in the family, full of good humour and popular among his companions, loving his numerous children dearly. Herbert was buried in the church graveyard at Chalfont St. Giles and prominent among the tributes were the wreaths sent by the Kent County Cricket Eleven. As a token of the great respect that his old club had for their former colleague, play was suspended for half an hour at Tonbridge during the match with Hampshire whilst the funeral was taking place.

Mary Ann was therefore left to bring up her large family on her own, and it says much for her character and determination that she managed to cope so well. This trait must have been passed on to her eldest child, Edith Minnie Hearne, who was still at school when her father died. Although Herbert rightly has his niche in the cricket records, it is his daughter and two grandchildren who have played such a prominent part in their family's story.

Several remarkable women form part of the Hearne family history, none more so than Edith. Born on 21st July 1887 at Chalfont St. Giles, Buckinghamshire, she became employed in the catering trade and subsequently emigrated to South Africa and continued in that line of business. In June 1916 she married William Henry Sturgess.

Her son Eric and daughter Irene have written the following tribute:-

"We had an interesting and rich family life. Sport played its role. Mother often spoke of the Hearnes and their cricketing prowess. We heard stories of her Uncle J.T.'s visits to India during the winter months to coach for the Maharajah of Patiala – a favourite was of how he sat in his bath to eat the large mangoes and the juice ran down to drip off his elbows into the bath!!

For our holidays at the coast Mother drove usually with 2 or 3 children distances of 500 to 700 miles on the untarred roads so that Eric could participate in the tennis tournaments taking place in other parts of the country, which he did from the age of 14.

In 1947 we were able to send Mother to England to see Eric play at Wimbledon, and in 1949 and 1950 she shared in the thrill of watching him win the Mixed Doubles Title in 1949 with Sheila Summers and in 1950 with Louise Brough. I shall never forget her joy and pride as we drove with Eric along the main drive at Wimbledon and heard the crowds lining that road, clapping and shouting "Come back next year, Eric!"

Herbert would have been even more proud of his grandson, Eric Sturgess, if he had seen also the young man's early cricket potential, as evinced by his batting performances; but, like many other youthful sportsmen he had to earn a living first, and consequently his studies to become a chartered accountant had priority. This was very much to the regret of Fred Burton (of Herts) who said "How can a man with Hearne blood in his veins give up cricket?"

Soon after leaving school (Parktown High) Eric Sturgess had to choose between tennis (he was the Transvaal Champion at the time), and cricket. In his first senior game for Old Parktonians he hit 104 off a strong Jeppe Old Boy's attack that included Norman Gordon, a future Test cricketer, but was out off the last ball of the day; later he represented a war-time Transvaal XI. Finding that cricket took up too much of his spare time Eric chose tennis, with happy results for himself and South Africa although his talents came very near to being lost altogether as the following account will show.

The war years saw Sturgess do an excellent flying job, firstly as an instructor, and then on operations with No. 4 S.A.A.F. Spitfire Squadron in Italy from February to October 1944 with the rank of captain. His unit was mainly engaged in dive bombing and strafing ground targets as there was very little German air activity in their part of Italy early in the autumn of 1944.

On the 20th October Eric spotted a German staff car on the road between Rimini and Imala. Diving to attack at 50 feet his Spitfire was hit in the engine from 20 mm anti-aircraft gunfire and immediately caught fire. Desperately climbing to about 800 feet he managed to roll the 'plane onto its back and dropped out of the cockpit; pulling the parachute ripcord immediately, he descended safely and was taken prisoner by the Germans. He was taken to Stalag Luft 3 in Germany where he remained until the end of January 1945 when, together with other prisoners, he was moved to Luckenwalde, some 20 miles south of Berlin.

Finally, after seven months as a prisoner of war, Eric was released by the advancing Russians and flown back to England when he took the opportunity to meet his grandmother, some of her sisters and numerous other members of the Hearne family. He also made a shaky first acquaintance with Wimbledon's grass tennis courts. He did not, however, entirely desert cricket, for he played a lot during World War II, including a match with Wally Hammond's R.A.F. team.

Herbert with his wife
Mary Ann and ten
of their children.

Eric Sturgess in
action at Wimbledon.

If South Africa lost a potential international cricket player, then their lawn tennis team gained one of their greatest. With his inherent natural ability Eric won the national singles eleven times and the doubles nine times. His international record is also a wonderful one: he won the Wimbledon mixed doubles twice, the United States doubles, the French mixed doubles and the British hard court singles, doubles and mixed doubles titles, to name a few of his achievements.

In 1948 he reached the men's singles final of the United States championships only to be beaten by Pancho Gonzales. After his retirement as a regular competitor Eric was appointed as a consultant and advisor to assist coaches throughout the country.

Irene Sturgess was no less prominent in the field of education than her brother was as a sportsman and she matriculated from Parktown Girl's High School in 1935. She obtained BSc (Hons), MSc and PhD degrees from the University of Witwatersrand, the Transvaal Teachers' Higher Diploma from the Johannesburg College of Education, and an Associateship from the Institute of Education of the University of London. She taught Science and Biology in various high schools in the Transvaal, and for seven years was Head of the Science Department of Parktown High School for Girls. Shortly after the war she returned to the University of Witwatersrand as a lecturer in Zoology to assist with the large number of ex-servicemen returning from World War II.

In 1988 Irene received a singular honour, the Johannesburg College of Education Gold Medal of Honour for Distinguished Service to Education. The award was first made in 1964 and since then 36 men and women have received a Gold Medal. Certain of the criteria for the award have changed slightly over the years, but the most important remain:

"The award shall be based on merit, irrespective of race, and shall be made for distinguished service to education in institutions ranging from pre-school to University".

Irene loved to visit England and meet her relatives; she took a keen interest in the development of this cricketers' history, and was always only too willing to assist with her wealth of South African knowledge. It is sad to relate that she died on 1st January 1990, not very long after a long holiday around England when she saw many friends and members of the Hearne family for the last time.

Chapter 12

Walter Hearne
(Kent 1887-1896)

WALTER, born 15th January 1864, was the second of the three brothers from Chalfont St. Giles who became professional cricketers.

He played his first match at Lord's on 9th May 1887 for Colts of the South *v* Colts of the North. Between 1887 and 1896 he played in 58 matches for Kent and scored 553 runs with an average of 7.57 and took 273 wickets for 15.93 each. 1887 was not an auspicious summer for two of Walter's cousins; Alec was very much off form, and G.G. did not play after July due to a sprained ankle. Frank, however, managed to come out third in Kent's batting averages with just over 29 runs an innings. This was Walter's first season with the Kent first eleven. He only played in five county matches, scoring a total of 73 runs and taking 4 wickets, but once again there were four Hearnes in the County team, and on at least one occasion they were the side's first four batsmen.

His short career is admirably summed up by W.A. Bettesworth in an article which appeared in *Cricket. A Weekly Record of the Game* on Thursday 9th June 1898:-

"One of the finest bowlers that ever the Kent committee was fortunate enough to discover, Walter Hearne was improving so rapidly year by year, that his future seemed to offer all sorts of possibilities. In 1893, he was at the top of the bowling averages in England, and although a broken finger kept him out of the field during part of the season, there can be no question that he quite deserved the honour. In the following year he took 116 wickets for 13 runs each. In the three consecutive matches against Surrey, Gloucestershire and Nottinghamshire he took thirty-eight wickets at an average of five runs apiece – a remarkable record".

In that year of 1894 Walter did indeed enjoy a very good season which might have been even better had the Kent fielding not been woefully inadequate. One of his best bowling performances was 6 for 37 and 7 for 24 against Gloucestershire at Blackheath in July. A few days later at Maidstone he took 5 for 29 and 7 for 43 against Nottinghamshire. Lancashire batsmen were his victims when he had 8 for 66 at Tonbridge. Wootton's benefit match at Catford Bridge when Kent played Surrey saw Walter take 7 for 46 and 6 for 52; other successful feats were 5 for 64 versus Warwickshire and 7 for 64 versus Somerset.

Whilst Walter had become a rising star in the Kent team, 1894 saw the County to all intents and purposes terminate the playing career of his cousin George Gibbons Hearne, a decision which some cricket pundits regarded as somewhat hasty.

The rapid advance of Walter as a first-class bowler virtually came to a halt in 1895 and the Kent attack was thus much weaker because of the serious gap this caused. Bettesworth goes on to say, "But, unhappily, after he had shown greater promise than ever in 1895, an accident to his knee practically put an end to his career as a first-class cricketer; it was an irreparable misfortune for his county. He is still able to bowl, and his services are highly valued as a coach. He has just finished an engagement at Harrow School".

When Crow, the Kent county scorer, gave up his duties, the position was offered to Walter Hearne, who was very pleased to accept it; he could now, to his great relief, still keep in touch with county cricket. In fact, he remained the Club scorer until his death in 1925. After the accident to his knee he was able to play in one or two county matches, but eventually it gave way again. The accident occurred when he was playing for St. Lawrence, Canterbury, against Westgate-on-Sea, and his own account is quoted in the same issue of *Cricket; A Weekly Record of the Game*:-

"While I was bowling, my knee gave way. I have always put it down to the long spikes which I was using. I used to come down very heavily on my heel, and then spin round. I think that the spikes must have been firmly fixed in the ground".

"You did not play again that season?"

"No. Not until the following season, when I thought that I had quite recovered after the long rest. Against Gloucestershire and Lancashire I was all right, but in the Yorkshire match I was batting with Mr. Marchant, who was in a scoring mood, and I was playing a better innings myself than I had ever done before, when I slipped in turning to run, and once more the mischief was done. When I broke down I had made 34, which was my highest innings in county cricket. I never could do much with the bat, and I recollect going in last to make 13 in one of the matches against Nottinghamshire. Of course, when I went to the wickets I intended to play a very careful game, but the second ball from Flowers was so tempting that I had a go at it and was caught right on the boundary."

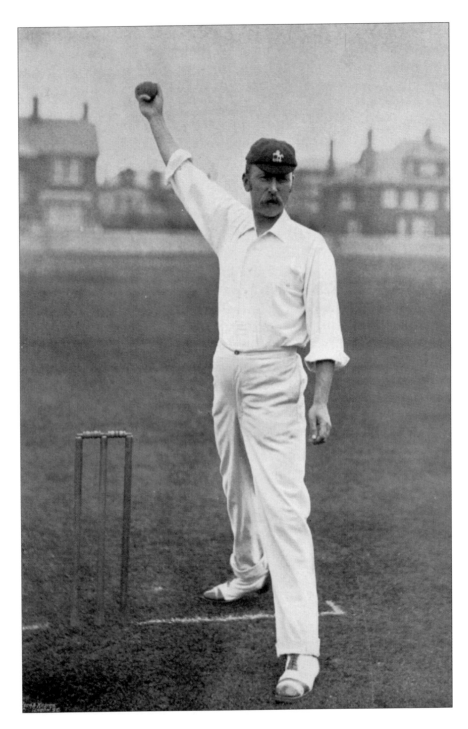

Kent at Catford 1893
back row: Umpire, W.Hearne, F.Martin, C.W.Little, W.Wright, Umpire Thoms
centre row: T.T.N.Perkins, J.Le Fleming, F.Marchant, L.Wilson, W.L.Knowles
front row: A.Hearne, G.G.Hearne

Walter Hearne
when he was the
Kent scorer.

"Is there any hope that your knee will be quite sound again?"

"It is possible that it may get well enough to allow me to go through another season or two, but I am getting older. I have never got my pace back. I have now to put my leg down in a manner which prevents this. Formerly I came down on my heel; now I have to use the toe, and get the pace from the shoulder."

It is not known where Walter resided during his early playing days at Canterbury, but he knew John Fagg, who was landlord of the *Bat and Ball* at that time, and his family; the *Bat and Ball* is located opposite the main entrance to the Canterbury ground. The 1881 census return lists John aged 32, a licensed victualler, his wife Hannah aged 30, two sons Arthur and Ernest J., a daughter Laura and Hannah's unmarried sister Eliza Ferryman who worked for them. Both Laura and her as yet unborn sister Emily Fagg were destined to have close cricket associations all their lives. After the death of her husband, Hannah Elizabeth Fagg continued to manage the *Bat and Ball* and then on 27th September 1892 she married Walter Hearne at St. Matthew's Church, Hammersmith. Walter's brother, John Thomas, was witness at the ceremony. They had two children, Henry Walter born October 15th 1893, who became Deputy Borough Treasurer for Bexley Borough Council, and Ethel. Both Ethel and her step-sister Laura remained spinsters and after the death of Walter they lived in Chalfont St. Giles with their uncle J.T. Hearne at Lynton Cottage. During the First World War Emily, whose first husband had died, remarried, into the cricketing world, her second husband being Frank Dutnall who played for Kent in 1919 and 1920 and who later had a successful career in Lancashire League cricket. His brother W.M. Dutnall also appeared for Kent.

After they retired from the *Bat and Ball*, Walter and Hannah went to live at Oaten Hill Place, a secluded little cul-de-sac off the junction of Dover Street and Oaten Hill, a short distance outside the Canterbury City walls. Walter died on 2nd April 1925, aged 61, at the Nursing Home in Ethelbert Road, following an operation, only two months after the death of his wife.

The obituary in the *Kentish Gazette* of 4th April 1925 sums up his character:-

"A thorough-going sportsman both on and off the field – genial, kindly, with a shrewd humour – Mr. Walter Hearne was held in the most affectionate regard by the Kent officials and players alike, by Lord Harris, Colonel Troughton, Captain W.S. Cornwallis, and all responsible for the government of Kent cricket, his services to the County were very highly valued. The team, who will feel his loss severely, always presented him with a token of their regard at the close of each season. Walter had a genius for attracting people, and in East Kent especially his death will be deeply mourned by a host of friends and admirers. As a cheery host of the *Bat and Ball* at Canterbury many years, he will be remembered".

Walter is generally described as a "cheery host" by his numerous friends and acquaintances, and appeared to them as a man with a very genial personality. This is probably correct; however, it must be said that there appears to have been another side to his character, for he was held in great awe by his family who indulged him and did most of the hard work especially as he was away with the County team for much of the summer.

Walter was not a particular favourite with at least one of his grand-daughters, whom he would upset by showing her the spoils of a day's rough shooting with his friends; in fact, she disliked visiting Canterbury when grand-father Walter was at home. Perhaps Walter was not at ease with children, but there is no doubt that he was extremely popular within his own circle.

It would be a very interesting conclusion to this chapter if I was able to say with any certainty that Walter's step-son, Arthur, was related to that fine Kent opening batsman Arthur Fagg, born in Chartham, who played for Kent between 1932 and 1957, but this relationship cannot be established.

Chapter 13

John Thomas Hearne
'J.T.' or 'Old Jack'
(Middlesex 1888-1923)

FOR many years the initials J.T. to countless thousands of cricket enthusiasts were sufficient to identify this remarkable player and they conjured up the mental picture of a tall, lithe bowler approaching the wicket with a wonderfully easy rhythm and a high delivery to match, pitching the ball on the proverbial sixpence. This is no real exaggeration for his success as one of the greatest medium paced bowlers was founded on his quite exceptional control and ability to perform for very long spells without seeming to show signs of strain or fatigue. He could bowl a good off break with finger spin or let the ball go with his arm, all disguised with skilful variations of speed of delivery so that batsmen found he could be virtually unplayable especially on bad wickets. He was also an excellent fieldsman and a much better batsman than has been acknowledged.

John Thomas was born at Chalfont St. Giles, Buckinghamshire, on 3rd May 1867, where he lived all his life. His father was William Hearne, a carpenter, undertaker and builder, and a very good club cricketer himself who had inherited the business from J.T.'s grandfather, Joseph Hearne. William died at Chalfont St. Giles on 17th July 1900 two days after his 80th birthday. It will thus come as no surprise to the reader to learn that J.T. was intended to follow in the family business as a carpenter. John Thomas had five brothers and two sisters; the eldest brother Henry became a schoolteacher; Joseph the second eldest followed his father's trade; William obtained a position as groundsman at the Household Brigade's ground, Chelsea, whilst Herbert and Walter became first class cricketers themselves and played for Kent CCC.

Chalfont St. Giles lies off the A413, the road from Chalfont St. Peter to Amersham, a short distance west of Rickmansworth. Turning off the main road by *The Pheasant*, down a short hill, one is confronted by a very pleasant village aspect of cottages and shops adjoining a green and a pond, with the fine old church in the background, a typical English scene which has not greatly changed over the past years, although much urban development has taken place on the outskirts of the village centre. Following the High Street to Dean Way leads to the old residence, Milton's Cottage, where the poet came in 1665 to escape the plague which was then rife in London.

J.T. attended the village school in School Lane, when Mr. Ford was the headmaster, followed by F. Register who took a keen interest in his promising pupil's career. He turned out for the village cricket club at the age of 14 under W. Curtis as captain when they played at Silsden Meadows. An account of a game played in July 1881 notes that "J. Hearne, a lad of 15, bowled with great skill and also made 10 very neatly". He also played well at soccer.

Cricket took over from carpentry and building, and when he was eighteen or nineteen years old he was appointed coach and groundsman at Evelyns School, Colham Green, Hillingdon, Middlesex, where G.T. Worsley the headmaster trained boys for entry into the public schools.

Worsley lived at Colham House, opposite the school, where the large gardens and greenhouses provided vegetables and decorative plants for the school grounds. He also owned a few cows in the vicinity which supplied the establishment with fresh milk and butter.

At that time the district around Colham Green was largely farmland and still quite rural in character. 'Evelyns', originally erected as a private house in about 1870, stood just off the north west corner of the junction of Colham Green Road and Falling Lane, with adjacent playing fields. The school was founded by the aforementioned G.T. Worsley, who added school buildings to the house in 1872, and remained there until 1931 when a move was made to Farnborough. For many years it was in the first rank of prep schools in the country. Pupils were prepared for Eton, Harrow, Charterhouse and Wellington, and many well-known and titled men attended. Among those who played cricket there were Lord Mildmay, Peter Cazalet and Lord Vansittart. The present Evelyns Secondary Modern School, a little to the west of the old site, perpetuates the name.

To reach Colham Green from Chalfont, J.T. travelled in the coach which ran from Banbury to London via Brackley, Buckingham, Winslow, Aylesbury, Wendover, Amersham, Uxbridge and Ealing; named 'The Union', the service was run by J. Hearn and Co., no less! Presumably he would have boarded the coach at *The Pheasant* corner, Chalfont, and alighted near the *Red Lion* in Hillingdon Village, walking the remainder of the journey via Royal Lane.

Cricket had some priority at Evelyns, where the headmaster, eager to foster local interest in the game, allowed Colham Green CC to play on the ground during summer holidays when they had the use of rooms in the house for tea. The club members were also allowed into evening practice during term time.

Under T.B. Hughes' guidance cricket was an important feature of games at Evelyns; in fact the Masters' eleven could hold their own against leading club teams. J.T. was soon recruited into the side and played four successive seasons for them from 1887 to 1890. His outstanding performances in early years were as a bowler, although in those days he was fairly slow. In 1887, against the Old Carthusians, he took 5 for 21 followed by 6 for 19 against Old Wykehamists. His best feats in those youthful days were 8 for 31 versus the Will-o'-the-Wisps, and the Old Carthusians suffered again when he took 7 of their wickets for 27 and in addition scored 27 not out.

While he was at Evelyns the headmaster W.E.W. Collins, a noted author and a fast bowler, encouraged the young man to bowl faster than hitherto, mainly because he did not believe his protégé would make the Middlesex XI as a slow bowler. Collins persuaded A.J. Webbe, the captain of Middlesex, to visit Evelyns on two separate occasions although J.T. performed poorly each time. However, Webbe had seen enough to be convinced that the talent was there and so in 1888, when he was 21 years old, J.T. was invited to play for Colts of Middlesex versus MCC. Although the weather was bad and largely spoiled his first real trial he did manage to take four wickets. The same year he was also given the opportunity to play for Middlesex against the Australians and took the wickets of Worrall and G.H.S. Trott for 19 runs in 11 overs, although he scored a duck in each innings.

Some have expressed surprise that he did not play any more first-class cricket until much later. This may be explained by the fact that when he was asked to play in the next match against Surrey one of his colleagues at Evelyns School pointed out that he was not qualified by residence. He, therefore, had no alternative but to decline, and went to live with his brother William at 21 Craven Cottages, West Kensington, for the necessary two-year qualifying period. He did, however, continue with his work and cricket at Evelyns School during the summer months.

One day in May 1890 a telegram arrived at the school, whilst J.T. was preparing the pitch, requesting him to turn out for Middlesex that very day. Hurrying to the local station, probably West Drayton or Hayes, to catch a train to Paddington, he read in the newspapers that Nottinghamshire, the County Champions, were to be his opponents at Lord's. The journey from Evelyns to Lord's seemed the longest he had ever made. The thrilling anticipation of actually playing in another first-class cricket match was marred by the anguish he felt knowing that he would be late. Many thoughts ran through his mind: perhaps he would not get such a wonderful chance again, and he wondered what Mr. Webbe would say. Fortunately the visitors were batting, but peace of mind did not come until Webbe, seeing him approaching the professionals' room, called out that it was all right but added that he had nearly been left out of the team. He promptly repaid Webbe's confidence by bowling so well that at the end of the first afternoon's play, Arthur Shrewsbury, arguably among the greatest batsmen of the time, congratulated him on his performance; and well he might, for in Notts' second innings Jack Hearne took 6 for 62, including the wickets of Shrewsbury, Scotton, Flowers and J.A. Dixon.

In his next match he took the wickets of both W.G. and E.M. Grace, and against the Australians he took a total of eight wickets for 91 runs (5 for 42 and 3 for 49); he had arrived at the forefront of first-class cricket.

Wisden commented that ". . . in young Hearne Middlesex possesses one of the most promising colts they have produced for some years and they will do well to persevere with him in the future".

From then onwards he remained a regular Middlesex professional until he retired in 1914, although he actually played his last match for the County in 1923 against Scotland when he was one of the oldest men to appear in first class cricket. Remarkably, he played for Middlesex from 1890 to 1914 without a break, except for missing two matches with a strained arm, and his playing career spanned 36 years with the Middlesex County team. Within three years of his 50th birthday he bowled with the same effortless grace even if the old deadly sting was not so apparent.

John Thomas Hearne's cricket developed rapidly. In 1891 in all first class matches he took 129 wickets for just over 11 runs apiece, heading the national bowling averages. His efforts went far to ensure an excellent season for Middlesex, who had been looking for a bowler of his calibre for some time. One of his most notable bowling performances took place in June of the 1891 season. On the 4th, 5th and 6th of that month Middlesex played Yorkshire at Lord's and on a wicket badly affected by rain Yorkshire made 109 and 77, J.T. taking 7 for 37 and 7 for 28. Middlesex could only reply with 63 and 54, J.T. bagging a pair.

A few days later, also at Lord's, he took 8 of the Lancashire first innings wickets for 22, all clean bowled, with 4 wickets in 6 balls at one point, just missing a hat trick.

Later on, towards the end of August, Middlesex had a drawn match at Nottingham thoroughly spoiled by rain. Nottinghamshire were bowled out for a meagre total of 84, due to some amazing bowling by J.T. who took 9 for 32.

NOTTINGHAMSHIRE *v* **MIDDLESEX**

at Nottingham on 27, 28, 29 August 1891

Match drawn

Nottinghamshire

First innings

W. Flowers	c Phillips	b Nepean	9
W. Gunn	c Stoddard	b Hearne	10
A. Shrewsbury		b Hearne	21
W. Barnes		b Hearne	14
Mr. R. Daft		b Hearne	0
T. Attewell	c Rawlin	b Hearne	3
Mr. C.W. Wright		b Hearne	8
H.B. Daft		b Hearne	0
W. Attewell	c Watson	b Hearne	6
F. Shacklock		not out	13
M. Sherwin		b Hearne	0
			84

Bowling:

Mr. Nepean	23-13-27-1
Hearne	40-22-32-9
Rawlin	21- 9-25-0

Second Innings:
22-2 wkts.

Middlesex

First Innings:

97

During those remarkable seasons he was bowling against great batsmen such as W.G. Grace, Tom Hayward, Bobby Abel, Ranjitsinhji, Johnny Tyldesley, C.B. Fry and many others. Lest it be thought that the pitches in those days were indifferent enough to favour the bowler, it must be said that by now much more attention was being given to their preparation in order to ensure a reasonable surface.

J.T. Hearne in 1891 became the first Middlesex bowler to take 100 wickets in a season. In his 16 matches for Middlesex he captured a total of 118 wickets at 10.39 runs apiece. With able support from Rawlin, the Middlesex attack ensured the County's third place in the championship. It is worth noting that 1891 marked the commencement of a run of eight consecutive seasons when he exceeded 100 wickets.

In 1891-92 J.T. toured South Africa with the England team and played in the only Test match. This took place at Cape Town and was the match in which Frank Hearne, appearing for South Africa, faced his two brothers and cousin J.T. in the England side. The other noteworthy feature is the fact that although England won easily by an innings, their batting was indifferent (G.G. Hearne collected a duck) until J.T., batting no. 10 and scoring 40, joined H. Wood. On this occasion the Surrey player made his only century in first class cricket, 134 not out.

J.T. loved to recount fond memories of overseas tours. He liked South Africa very much, and would tell of very exciting journeys over the wild veldt in coaches pulled by ten horses and mules, with black drivers cracking their long whips over the lead animals. It all sounded romantic to his young relatives but no doubt was really very arduous.

In 1894 the Maharaja of Patiala, a very keen sportsman, invited J.T. to visit his country during the winter in order to improve the standard of native cricketers.

Who's Who In India states: "The Maharaja ranked first in the precedence list of Native States in India and enjoyed a salute of 17 guns. In the early 1890's when the Punjab and the plains of the Ganges constituted the heart of British India, the Maharaja Sir Rajendra Singh brought out the Englishmen Brockwell and J.T. Hearne to coach, and built in the grounds of his palace at Patiala a stately cricket oval as well as another, an all-weather ground, at Chail, his summer residence in the Simla hills. Sir Rajendra died in 1900, aged 28. His son Bhupinder Singh continued his love of the game of cricket and presented the 'Ranji' trophy for the cricket championship of India".

The acquaintance of J.T. and the Maharaja was renewed when the Prince came to stay at 'The Vache', which was then a private country house on the outskirts of Chalfont St. Giles, now occupied by Coal Board Management. The friendship between the two men, both so devoted to cricket, resulted in Jack continuing his trips to India during the winters of 1895-96 and 1899-1900. His inclusion in the Australian tour of 1897-98 meant that he could not go that year. One match during these Indian visits is worth mentioning. It concerns a game played at Umballa in 1899 between MCC and Ground and the Rest of India, organised by Sir F.A. Robertson, I.C.S. The MCC team was selected from members resident in India and J.T. represented the Ground staff. MCC won easily by 159 runs due partly to the 16 wickets taken by J.T., but primarily, and this is the unusual feature, to his batting high in the order and scoring 121 runs.

From 1890 to 1897 J.T. achieved a remarkable sequence of bowling

performances. Over these eight seasons he amassed a total of 1,485 wickets at an average of barely 16 runs per wicket. Those vintage years contained some phenomenal feats of bowling; for instance, in 1896 he took his hundredth wicket on 12th June, and finished the season with a total of 257 wickets, then a record haul in a single year. J.T.'s outstanding performance in 1896 must be his bowling for MCC and Ground versus the Australians at Lord's on 11th and 12th June, when after scoring 219, MCC dismissed their opponents for 18 in their first innings. J.T. took 4 for 4 whilst A.D. Pougher had 5 wickets for 0 runs, G. Giffen the eleventh man being absent in both Australian innings. When Pougher commenced bowling there was 18 on the board for just 3 wickets, and incredibly no addition was made to this meagre total. The Australians did better in their second knock, scoring 183, J.T. taking all their 9 wickets for 73. It is idle speculation, but had Giffen batted he might well have captured all 10. In what must be a masterpiece of understatement, *Wisden*, commenting on the tourists' second innings, stated:- ". . . and J.T. Hearne again bowled splendidly".

The Australians were, not unnaturally, very impressed with their redoubtable opponent's performances but thought he might not be such a thorn in their flesh on Australian wickets, and to some degree they were correct, although J.T. did claim his fair share of victims when England visited Australia in 1897-98. During the next Australian tour in 1899 however, John Thomas achieved a unique feat in the third Test at Leeds on 30th June, when he performed the hat trick, taking the prize wickets of Hill, Noble, and Gregory – all dismissed for ducks. One of the umpires was William Hearne.

1896 saw many personal triumphs for J.T.; against Yorkshire at Lord's on 21st, 22nd and 23rd May, he took 7 for 104 in a Yorkshire innings of 381 (J.T. Brown 208). Against Somerset on 25th and 26th May – Rawlin's Benefit Match – Middlesex scored 396 (Stoddart 121); in reply, Somerset could only manage 179 and 106 due to some devastating bowling by J.T. who took 6 for 47 and 6 for 44. In this same year he took the first hat trick of his career.

'Jack' Hearne backed up his season of brilliant bowling with some valuable tail-end scores of 20 or more runs, for it must not be forgotten that he was more than just a useful batsman, and could keep his end going very effectively when the occasion demanded.

After reaching third place in the championship table in 1896, Middlesex fell back to equal seventh with Warwickshire the next season, due mainly to the lack of another first-class bowler to support J.T. Hearne who was bearing the brunt of the county's attack with consistent success. Support was forthcoming from Albert Trott, the Australian, who had migrated to England following his omission from the Australian touring side of 1896 and who became qualified to play for Middlesex in 1898. In Trott's first season both he and J.T. took over 100 wickets and Middlesex rose to second place behind Yorkshire.

The Gentlemen *v* Players match of that year played at Lord's in July was a momentous occasion for it was also the fiftieth birthday of the legendary W.G. Grace. The Champion scored 43 when he opened the Gentlemen's first innings and 31 not out batting low in the order for his second knock due to a badly bruised heel. J.T. had very good performances with the ball – 5 for 87 and 6 for 65.

The Gents had replied manfully to the Players' first innings of 335 (Gunn 139) with 303, but were well short in their second effort mustering only 158 to the Players 263.

In 1899 Middlesex were second again and Trott became the first player to make over 1,000 runs and capture 200 wickets in a season. J.T., however, had very little success that year. Perhaps his best performance was against Somerset at Lord's in the May Bank Holiday match, which he and Trott won for Middlesex, bowling on a wicket badly affected by rain.

The summer of 1900 was a poor season for Middlesex, and with an out-of-form J.T. they fell back to equal seventh with Gloucestershire and Surrey in the table. Although J.T. generally was not at his best, he still managed to take a total of 96 wickets for Middlesex and to do very well on occasions, particularly against Surrey. In the encounter at the Oval, Surrey looked all set for victory with Middlesex needing 18 runs with nine second-innings wickets down; however, facing a fearsome Lockwood, J.T. proved his batting ability, seeing his side through to victory. 1900 was also noteworthy for J.T.'s benefit match against Sussex at Lord's when A.E. Stoddart played his last first-class game and scored a magnificent 221.

The following season J.T. was again off form, and the fact that he only took 52 wickets at an average of over 30 runs each illustrates how far he had fallen from his normally high standard. He was virtually written off by some critics. Against the old enemy Surrey he took no wickets at all when they made 303 and 322, but his 7 for 55 in the second Essex innings saw Middlesex win their final game in a successful summer when they were again second to Yorkshire.

Unpredictable as ever, Middlesex failed to repeat their championship challenge in 1902 when they fell to twelfth position at the end of the season. It was a wet summer, which did not suit J.T., for although he was bowling more like his old self he could not make as much use of the slow wickets as he might have done a few years earlier. He took 61 wickets for Middlesex at 20.73 runs apiece, and finished fourth in the county bowling averages.

In June J.T. achieved the hat trick against Essex at Lord's when he took four wickets in five balls. He bowled as well as he had ever done in the Lord's match against Yorkshire when he took 6 for 39 and ensured Middlesex's first victory over the northerners for three years.

There has always been speculation about the cause of the short hiatus in the phenomenal consistency of J.T. Hearne's bowling: some have suggested that, for a man of over thirty, bearing the brunt of the Middlesex attack continually for a dozen years was taking its toll, and others argue more plausibly that it was the year or two of slow wickets which did not assist his style of bowling, and which coincided with a not unusual loss of form which may occur for short periods in the long careers of most professional cricketers.

1903 saw an astonishing advance in fortune for Middlesex. J.T. returned to something like his old form, bowling with his characteristic deadly accuracy and to such good purpose that he took 76 wickets for the county at less than 18 runs apiece.

Two of his successful efforts stand out; against Yorkshire at Lord's he took 6 for 39 and 4 for 75 whilst he and Trott bowled unchanged versus Lancashire when J.T. had 6 for 36 and Trott 4 for 69. Unfortunately rain spoiled the match after Lancashire were all out for 115 and Middlesex had made 53 for 2.

The fact that the summer of 1903 was again extremely wet does not entirely support the contention that J.T. was not so effective under such conditions, and his advance in this year made a substantial contribution toward Middlesex winning the County Championship. This season they fielded a fine, well-balanced team with their batsmen supporting the splendid bowling with a succession of high scores. In a very exciting match at the Oval on 27th and 28th August, which Middlesex had at least to draw in order to win the Championship, J.T. and Albert Trott bowled out Surrey in their first innings for 57 with 4 for 26 and 6 for 19 respectively so that they had to follow on and with Wells bowling excellently in the second innings, Middlesex enjoyed a comfortable victory.

One match which illustrates how Middlesex replied to the criticism that they were lucky to stave off the challenge of Yorkshire in the race for the Championship was their game as Champion County versus The Rest of England at the Oval. After a slender lead of 46 on the first innings they declared their second innings closed at 254 for the loss of 8 wickets. Confidence in the Middlesex attack of Hearne, Trott, J.H. Hunt and Wells was completely justified when they bowled out a team of Test Match players for 184 in the first innings but the game ended in a draw.

Had Middlesex begun their defence of the Championship in 1904 as well as they played later in the season, they might well have finished above their eventual fourth place, as they were still a very fine team. J.T. Hearne was once again in good form, reserving some of his best bowling for matches at Lord's, always his favourite ground; he was described as a "Lord's man", probably because he took so many wickets on that famous turf, or because it was thought that he had a special affection for the majestic ground and its aura of authority. In fact, he enjoyed playing at Lord's more than at any other ground for the simple reason that he could so easily return to his beloved home and garden at Chalfont St. Giles, "just to see everything is in order", as he used to say.

On that ground, early in May, Middlesex scored 370 against Somerset who were dismissed for 126 and 125, J.T. taking 8 for 49 and 7 for 44. Early in June he took 4 for 37 (Trott 4-7) and 6 for 48 versus Yorkshire. His county bowling figures for the season were 83 wickets at 16 runs each.

J.T. also had a rather extraordinary season with the bat, and was well placed in the averages with 32.28 to his credit, although he only scored 226 runs. Going in last in most games, he was not out 18 times, which explains his somewhat flattering figures, although one must not overlook the fact that he was a really capable batsman as his performance against Yorkshire at Sheffield illustrates. More, batting number 10, helped Bosanquet put on 128 in 48 minutes. With Bosanquet's dismissal J.T. arrived at the crease, whereupon he and More proceeded to add 91 for the last wicket in 52 minutes.

J.T. did not have much success in the next two years in an inconsistent Middlesex side, although in 1905 he took eight Essex wickets for 93, out of a total of 268, and then went on to make his highest score of 56 when he and Tarrant put on 98 in an unfinished ninth wicket stand.

1906 was a dismal season. Middlesex could once again only manage eleventh place in the table and poor J.T., at very low ebb, scraped a meagre 34 wickets at a costly 30.8 runs apiece.

The next year heralded a new era of success for Middlesex, skippered most of the time by Pelham Warner, who was fortunate to have a hard core of professionals who served him admirably. Towards the end of the period from 1907 until the outbreak of the First World War, there were Tarrant, Murrell, Hendren, H.W. Lee, J.T. Hearne and J.W. Hearne and Warner also was at his best. In 1907 Tarrant made a great contribution securing his first double for Middlesex. Trott did reasonably well again with 48 wickets and two hat tricks in the same innings during his benefit year and J.T. took 56 at 17.41.

At Manchester, against Lancashire, he took 5 for 38 and 6 for 29 ensuring an innings win for Middlesex. He followed this immediately at Trent Bridge with 7 for 42 and 3 for 29 but could not stave off a five-wicket victory by Nottinghamshire.

1908 saw the introduction of Patsy Hendren into a powerful batting side and the 'phantom' appearance of Thomas John Hearne against the Philadelphians at Lord's. The following wet season was significant if only for one reason, and that was the introduction of J.W. Hearne, a relative of J.T., into the Middlesex eleven. Tarrant did the double again, and Plum Warner made an undefeated 127 against the Australians out of Middlesex's 307 for five. J.T. took 51 county wickets at an average of 25, well above Tarrant's 17.23. The following season, 1910, apparently determined to show his young cousin that he was still the master, he headed the English bowling averages at the age of 44, and for Middlesex he captured 116 wickets at 12 runs each. Against Gloucestershire at Lord's on 27th and 28th June he and Tarrant bowled unchanged in both innings taking 12 for 70 and 8 for 59 respectively.

1911 was a kind season for batsmen and there were some prolific scores by Middlesex, who were third in the table. Hendren made his first hundred for the County whilst J.W. Hearne, who scored 234 not out against Somerset, had become one of the leading all-round cricketers. J.T., who seemed to be going on for ever, was the foremost bowler, taking 108 wickets at an average of 18.09 for the County and 122 at 17.49 in all first class matches.

The numerous wet pitches of the following summer did not suit batsmen and the season was one of very low scores; it is therefore not surprising that bowling feats took precedence. J.T. and Tarrant dismissed Surrey for 67 at the Oval in a drawn game. In the return match at Lord's the same two Middlesex bowlers put them out for 52, J.T. 5 for 18 and Tarrant 5 for 28. Middlesex themselves could only manage 74 in their own first innings in another draw. J.T.'s county bowling average was 15.59 (he did the hat trick against Warwickshire) followed closely by J.W. (who had a very moderate season with the bat) with an average of 16.76.

The claims of the First World War in 1914 may have deprived a fine Middlesex side of a championship which would have been a fitting end to the long career of J.T., who was still in tip-top form with a bowling average similar to that of the younger Jack Hearne. Although 1914 was to all intents and purposes the final season for J.T., he did make one appearance again in 1923, when he was 56 years of age, for Middlesex against Scotland scoring 20 in his only innings and taking 6 for 64 in the match.

Until Fred Titmus claimed his 2,000th victim in 1968, J.T. was the only Middlesex bowler to have reached this total. Many other examples of John Thomas Hearne's bowling achievements during his career could be quoted; suffice to say that in 15 seasons he took over 100 wickets, in 3 seasons more than 200, besides which he scored 7,137 runs for an average of 11.04 and he

*John Thomas Hearne's
batting stance*

John Thomas Hearne's bowling action

*John Thomas with
his wife Edith Anna*

held 382 catches mostly close to the wicket. His total of wickets was 3,061 (av. 17.75). J.T. bowled, for much of his career, for a Middlesex side under enormous strain from a lack of first class bowling support. There was no better bowler of his type. With his easy rhythm and action he achieved a consistent length with the minimum of apparent effort, an asset which enabled him to bowl continuously for long stretches.

J.T. and J.W. maintained a close friendship, the high spot being an annual golf match at Chalfont, when the author frequently acted as caddy until the late 1930's. It has often seemed a great pity that J.T. did not have any children of his own, for he dearly loved his very numerous nieces and nephews, and was called upon to extricate some of the boys from difficult situations on more than one occasion. One favourite lad put himself beyond J.T.'s assistance when he tragically shot himself.

He was employed as a groundsman/coach of a well known London sports club whose secretary wrote to the coroner praising the dead man's character. The secretary was none other than A.E. Stoddart, the great Middlesex and England batsman, who ironically was to kill himself with a gun less than a year after the inquest on J.T.'s nephew.

It appeared for a long time that he would happily continue his life as a bachelor and it was something of a surprise to members of his family that he married in 1905 at the age of 38. His wife was Edith Anna Bowyer, born 21st October 1854 at 8 Sion Place, Bath, the residence of her father William Jeeves Bowyer, gentleman, later Colonel Bowyer. It is a family legend that Edith saw J.T. playing in a cricket match and thereupon decided that he was the man she was going to marry. The ceremony took place on Saturday 14th October 1905 in the parish church of Ashbrittle, a small village to the west of Wellington on the border of Somerset and Devon, the bride's family having settled there some time before. William Brockwell, the Surrey batsman who had long been a close friend, acted as J.T.'s best man. They had both been on the 1891-92 tour to South Africa, which was J.T.'s first trip abroad, and had together made winter visits to Patiala at the behest of the Maharaja.

There is no doubt that Edith Bowyer was a woman with a strong character, a fact well remembered by Hilda Garrard, who is a grand-daughter of J.T.'s brother Herbert and who has lived virtually a stone's throw from J.T.'s home all her life. The author has to thank her for much of the past history of the Chalfont branch of the Hearne family. Edith was also a well-connected and wealthy woman, and above all a keen cricket player who organised her own ladies' team under the name of Nausica. Exploits of her team appear in the scorebook of that famous women's cricket club founded in 1887, the White

Heather. Appearing initially as Miss Bowyer and later as Mrs. Hearne, Edith seems to have put herself in as opening bat but with little success! It is in keeping with her character that she obviously believed in leading from the front whatever the consequences.

Many famous names appear in the White Heather score book, such as the Hon. S. Hood, Miss Somerset, Miss Hoare, the Hon. Mrs. Bevan, Miss Leveson-Gower; for Nausica, Miss V. Twining, Miss H. Sickel, Miss W. Langridge and Miss A. Ogilvy. Mrs. Stanley Baldwin was also a member of the White Heather club.

Whatever may be said, one thing is absolutely certain: no woman was more devoted to her husband's career than Edith Anna, and J.T.'s longevity in first class cricket was due in no small measure to her support and devotion. She accompanied him to as many matches as possible, and the two were to be seen cycling (in Edith's case it was a tricycle) the four miles from their home to the station whenever he was playing at Lord's or near London. He was always a home-loving man who could not bear to be away any longer than necessary.

During World War I Edith gave most of her time to the men who were convalescent after having been wounded on active service, working in the canteen at the 3rd Australian General Hospital at Harefield.

On Anzac Day, 25th April, each year a memorial service is held at the picturesque church burial ground of Harefield, where so many Australian and New Zealand soldiers lie at rest. On Armistice Day, 11th November 1918, all the patients in the military hospital signed an 'Armistice Wheel' ward by ward.

After the War ended, Edith turned her energy to the benefit of the village ex-service men. The hospital referred to was a temporary wartime establishment in the grounds of a large private house, Harefield Park. Subsequently a Sanatorium was built on the site and has become the modern hospital well-known for the heart transplant surgery carried out by Dr. Magdi Yacoub and his team.

In the early years of their marriage J.T.'s wife, besides being an active cricketer, was also a member of both the Surrey and Somerset Clubs. Up to the outbreak of war she organised an annual charity match on the Ealing CC ground against her husband's team of men, the latter playing left-handed.

Edith's spirit contributed to her tragic death, for returning from London by train one foggy evening she alighted at the local station, Gerrards Cross, to find the fog was much worse and no conveyance available. Her husband, upon noting the impossible conditions outside, assumed that she would have stayed with her friends in town and retired for the night. Edith, however, in her determined way, decided to walk home and got hopelessly lost on

Goldhill Common. As a result of prolonged exposure she caught a chill and within a few days died of pneumonia on 5th December 1921.

John Thomas Hearne, under engagement at Lord's from 1891 to 1924, received £500 from MCC in lieu of a benefit match, whereas Middlesex granted him this favour with the Somerset game in 1900. In 1920 he received the honour of being elected a member of the Middlesex County Cricket Club committee. Until then William Gunn of Nottinghamshire had been the only cricket professional to be so honoured.

In the early 1920's, during the Easter vacation, J.T. coached at The Hoo, Hertfordshire, the home of the Hon. David Brand, later Viscount Hampden, who was a great friend of the late Sir G.O. ('Gubby') Allen.

In his early 60's he coached at Oxford before the start of the season, where he became immensely popular, and several university undergraduates, after achieving fame in various walks of life, have recalled their time with J.T. with pleasure and warmth.

After his retirement J.T., known affectionately by local folk as 'the squire of St. Giles', took an active interest in local affairs. He was a member of the Parish Council and the School Managers for several years; he was a church-warden for the Parish Church, and was a member of the local St. Giles Cricket Club and several others in the district. He had been a crack shot in his day, and would proudly show visitors the hunting trophies, mainly from India, which adorned the walls of his home 'Lynton Cottage' a few doors away from 'Milton's Cottage'. At 'Lynton Cottage' he built up a wonderful collection of British moths, tended his garden with great enjoyment, and provided a comfortable home for his niece Ethel Hearne, daughter of J.T.'s brother Walter, and her stepsister Laura Fagg and his widowed sister Annie.

Of the numerous cricketer Hearnes, and they have all been much loved and respected men, none has been held in more affection by his colleagues, friends, and family than John Thomas. This was revealed clearly to the author whilst researching J.T.'s life when more distant relatives, not quite conversant with their precise connection, would invariably look at the 'family tree' and say, "Where is J.T. on there? I knew him, such a gentleman". They could immediately pinpoint their own branch and relate this to John Thomas. He died on 17th April 1944 and Chalfont St. Giles lost a great cricketer, a great friend, a great villager and a great Christian. An earlier writer, when describing J.T.'s bowling, wrote of him as a man:

". . . who has been classical and as near perfect as a man can be in his command of such a thing as a cricket ball. This he has endowed with life. No cricketer, be he paid or unpaid, has ever been more of a gentleman on the field or off it. He has a quiet charm all his own and has lived with such devotion to his craft that he has always been fit for any struggle".

He lived the life of a country gentleman who preferred a sylvan retreat to urban life. His brother professionals honoured him for his quiet speech and gentle manner. He died in the village in which he was born and was buried in the parish churchyard near the grave of his brother Herbert, and on that day the flags at Lord's were flown at half-mast for one of cricket's greatest sons.

J.T.Hearne at Eton in 1917.

Chapter 14

John William Hearne
(Middlesex 1909-1936)

IT WILL come as a surprise to many to learn that John William, the finest cricketer in the family, and at the peak of his career arguably the equal of the best all-rounders in the country, was by and large self-taught.

His father, John Herbert Hearne, came from a long family line of wheelwrights, and was born at Chalfont St. Peter, Buckinghamshire. In his younger days John Herbert had been a useful underhand bowler but no batsman; a look at old records of his scores indicates that he seems to have made more "ducks" than most of his family put together! He often remarked that in those days keenness for the sport was so great that sometimes after a hard day's work the team would either walk or cycle to a match many miles away, unless of course they were lucky enough to borrow a van from one of the farmers. Being related to the famous family of Hearne cricketers his one ambition was to see his son play for the County and for MCC, and he would often steal a considerable amount of working time to give young John William bowling practice in the yard.

John William Hearne was born on the 11th February 1891 at York Villas, Waterloo Road, Uxbridge, which is now within the London Borough of Hillingdon. York Villas were a pair of tall old Victorian houses, now demolished, which used to stand on the western side of Waterloo Road towards the southern end; one of the houses was the home of John William's maternal grandparents who moved there from St. John's Road. As was the custom in those days, expectant mothers would undergo their confinement at their mothers' homes, where they could be properly looked after; thus, J.W. was actually born in Uxbridge and not at his parents' home in Harlington, as several writers have stated.

J.W.'s mother Rosina (née Richardson) had two sisters and five brothers. The boys were all keen sportsmen and several saw military service in the Boer War. There was then a voluntary military unit in Uxbridge where the recruits received some military instruction and rifle practice. Rosina herself was not to be left out and somehow or other achieved a remarkable proficiency as a markswoman, a fact that one of her grandsons was later to discover to his cost

*John William as a small boy
with his father.*

As a young man.

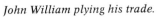

John William plying his trade.

when he challenged her to a target shooting match with his airgun. As the elder sister of several sporting brothers, it was only natural that she should take an interest in their activities, and Rosina was a keen follower of local cricket and football, acquiring a profound knowledge of the games. If she had lived today, she would doubtless have become an excellent sportswoman.

It was against this background of active, sports loving and industrious families that the young man grew up. It is therefore not difficult to understand that although he soon became a proficient craftsman at his father's trades, he developed a fondness for an outdoor sporting life at an early age, together with a keen knowledge of the countryside which he later passed on to his own two sons.

He was educated at Heston House School, Heston, Middlesex, located on the north west junction of Cranford Lane with Vicarage Farm Lane. These early formative years at Heston House School saw John William gradually becoming an excellent cricketer, topping the school averages for both batting and bowling. During his last year at school he took 61 wickets for 124 runs and eventually he appeared in local cricket for Harlington Cricket Club. By then he had become the lifelong friend of Sydney Heyward, who later farmed Manor Farm, Harlington. An even closer friend was Alfred Newman of Lansdowne House, next to the Church of St. Peter and St. Paul in the village. Sadly, Alfred was to lose his life in the First World War.

As a youth John William took part in 'beating the bounds' along with other Harlington lads. Whilst proceeding along Dawley Road he caught the eye of Violet Mary Benn whose mother ran a small shop and dairy whilst her father and brothers looked after the dairy farm. The attraction was mutual and they were eventually married after the close of the 1913 cricket season at St. Peter and St. Paul's Church on 27th September, when J.W.'s boyhood friend Alfred Newman was his best man. One of the young bridesmaids was Kate Ellen Hearne whose parents had emigrated to South Africa towards the end of the last century. The bride's father, James Benn, was a somewhat formidable man whom many folk, including his own family, found more than a little intimidating. Strangely enough, he always had respect for his new son-in-law, not for his achievements at cricket but because the younger man was the better shot with a 12-bore.

In 1906 John William joined the Lord's staff as a ground boy. His father's cousins George Francis, J.T. and Tom Hearne, who was then head groundsman at Lord's, had doubtless all been told of J.W.'s great promise. The young lads on the staff in those days were employed in selling score cards, cleaning and sweeping the ground and pushing the heavy roller; they were also expected to bowl in the nets when required. Two of J.W.'s young colleagues at that time were Harry Lee and Patsy Hendren's younger brother Jack who was killed in the First World War. These three boys were very close companions and the stories of their many escapades and brushes with Authority had more than a grain of truth. Several of these adventures are recounted by Harry Lee in his book, *Forty Years of English Cricket*.

Sometimes, when he managed to get an afternoon off, young Jack played for the Uxbridge Primrose League and on one occasion, against Hillingdon Court, he knocked up a century and rounded off the game by bowling the Hon. C.T. Mills who had scored 99.

During his younger days he played cricket for Uxbridge in one or two matches, but never had much success. He also played soccer for Uxbridge for several seasons, usually on the left wing where, as he said, he was out of the way of any 'rough stuff'.

One incident in those early carefree days on the ground staff at Lord's was remembered vividly. Soon after commencing work, the young John William Hearne was summoned before the Authorities who informed him in no uncertain terms that his bearing a well-known name in the cricket world cut no ice and only players of potential Test Match standard were of interest. He never forgot this and when, not too long after this incident, he had made his name as one of the finest all-round players, he often hoped that the gentlemen referred to also recalled their words.

Sometimes, when a large number of members engaged bowlers at the practice nets, the ground boys or the Middlesex colts were pressed into service and they could find themselves bowling to very prominent men. On one occasion, the Speaker of the House of Commons, the Rt. Hon. Lowther, surprised the Lord's staff by appearing for net practice at what was considered the early hour of 11 a.m. Young J.W. was the only bowler available and he so pleased the Speaker with his skill that a request was made for him to go and play cricket at the Cumberland home of the Rt. Hon. gentleman.

In 1909 J.W., together with H.W. Lee, was playing for the Cross Arrows and J.W. won a pair of batting gloves in that year for taking a hat-trick. During the period in which he played for the Cross Arrows he also won prizes for his batting; for instance, while only 16 years old he scored 137 not out against Paddington and District and 167 not out versus G.N. Loco, having had an average of 96 over the month, and taking 36 wickets for 7 runs each.

John William showed such early promise as an all-round player both before and during the time that he was on the Lord's ground staff that it is not surprising that he won his first county trial in 1909, at the age of 18. J.W.'s first appearance for the County was against Gloucestershire at Lord's on 17th and 18th May 1909 when Middlesex won by 1 wicket, J.W. scoring 2 and 5. Altogether he played in 8 games for Middlesex during 1909, with modest results.

The next season he made two centuries and bowled very well, particularly against Essex at Lord's when he took 7 wickets for only 2 runs in 5 overs and one ball. From then on his career rapidly developed and during the period before and just after World War One he was among the finest all-rounders in the country.

His first overseas tour was in the winter of 1910-11, when under the name of MCC a team of only eleven players sailed in the RMSP *Clyde* on 18th January for the West Indies. The *Clyde* was a graceful three-masted vessel with two of the masts aft of the two funnels and having an overhanging prow with a bowsprit, presenting an altogether regal appearance. The team was a weak one with only three first class professionals, but they managed to win two matches against the West Indies, the third being drawn. J.W. was quite successful, particularly with the ball, taking a total of 67 wickets.

His next trip was in 1911-12 when he was included in the official MCC tour of Australia after an outstanding season with Middlesex, which included an innings of 234 not out against Somerset at Lord's that still stands as a Middlesex record for the youngest player to reach a double century. The voyage started from Tilbury docks on 29th September 1911 on the S.S. *Orvieto*, a 12,000-ton liner of the Orient Line coaling at Port Said and Colombo en route, a dirty and unpopular necessity in the days of solid-fuel steamships. The team arrived at Adelaide on Saturday 4th November, having played a match against Ceylon at Colombo which they won easily.

The *Orvieto*, in common with many other large steamships, saw active service during World War I. She was used as a troop transport in 1914, a mine layer in 1915 and in 1916 she was an auxiliary cruiser with the 10th Cruiser Squadron.

The selection of J.W. was a great surprise to many people, especially the Middlesex Committee, who felt that the tour would be too onerous for a young man not yet 21 years old. However, although the views of Pelham Warner, the tour captain, prevailed, J.W.'s bowling in Australia proved a great disappointment.

In his book *England v Australia* (1912) Warner comments on J.W.'s bowling: ". . . Hearne was a great failure. Look at his Test Match average! He seldom struck a length and was very expensive, but whenever he did happen to get a length he worried the batsmen . . ."

It could be argued that the opinion of the Middlesex Committee was correct; perhaps Warner was unduly optimistic about his young protégé's entry into the Australian arena. To expect him to continue the form he had so rapidly achieved in County Cricket at home was asking a lot from a relatively inexperienced player.

In his first Test Match against Australia at Sydney J.W. went into bat at No. 6 with only a quarter of an hour before the close of play on the Saturday afternoon, and England not doing very well. Before a crowd of some 35,000 he coolly played out time and eventually went on to make a fine 76, followed by 43 in the second innings, not good enough to save the match, England losing easily.

The greatest triumph for J.W. was in the first innings of the second Test Match at Melbourne when he made a magnificent 114, giving only one possible chance to Armstrong in the slips at 77. Warner was full of praise and reckoned that at this point of the tour J.W. was batting far better than any of his colleagues.

At the age of 20 years 324 days, J.W. became and remained the youngest English player to score a Test century until Denis Compton made 102 for England *v* Australia in 1938 when only 20 years and 19 days old.

Pelham Francis (Plum) Warner took over the captaincy of Middlesex in 1908. Many young cricketers of Warner's era owe much of their successful careers to him, none more so than John William Hearne, who was held in high esteem by his county captain. Warner once referred to him as "my cricketing godson." He did in fact become godfather to J.W.'s first son in 1915.

Shortly after his marriage, John William went on his third overseas trip, the 1913-14 MCC tour of South Africa, the team sailing in the Union Castle Line R.M.S. *Saxon*, a two-funnel liner of nearly 13,000 tons. Although he made several very good scores, including a couple of centuries, and finished third in the batting averages behind J.B. Hobbs and J.W.H.T. Douglas, his bowling was not exceptional, the best effort probably being 5 for 49 in South Africa's first innings of the third Test Match at Johannesburg, which England won by 91 runs.

At the end of the 1914 cricket season J.W., together with the Australian Frank Tarrant, another great all-rounder for Middlesex, received an invitation from the Maharajah of Patiala to spend the winter playing and coaching for his state team. As the war with Germany was initially expected to be of short duration the cricketers readily accepted the chance to visit India with their wives.

Although the women enjoyed the hospitality that such an opportunity offered, there is no doubt that their husbands had more varied entertainment. J.W. in particular was in his element as he was able to exercise his skills with rod and gun to great advantage and he took part in big-game hunts as well as undertaking solo forays with his own tracker, in much the same way that J.T. had done in former years. Of course there were drawbacks, such as being awakened before the crack of dawn by a servant saying that the Maharajah was commanding Hearne sahib to go with him on a duck shoot. When recounting these experiences J.W. was wont to point out dryly that perhaps this was a little revenge for the fact that he had clean bowled the Maharajah for 0 at Lord's when he was captain of All India *v* M.C.C. during their first tour of England in 1911.

If there was a house party or some such gathering, etiquette demanded that nobody should leave before their royal host. This was all very well, but proceedings were apt to continue well into the small hours and the cricketers were expected to be up bright and fresh at their usual time, a fact seemingly overlooked by the eminent person who had no such obligation. It is likely that J.W. would have spent a longer period in India but the excessive heat was affecting his wife who by then was expecting their first child. Moreover, the course of the war looked ominous and rumours were rife about attacks on shipping by German surface raiders, given credence by the exploits of the cruiser *Emden* which had sunk numerous Allied vessels in the Bay of Bengal and the Indian Ocean between August and November 1914 before being eliminated by H.M.A.S. *Sydney* at the Cocos Islands.

They decided therefore to leave India as soon as possible and obtained passages on the ill-fated *Egypt*, which was sunk in a collision in the Bay of Biscay seven years later with a large loss of life and an enormous cargo of bullion. The return journey to England was uneventful until they reached the approaches to the English Channel when, due to what proved to be a false alarm, the ship altered course violently on account of a suspected enemy submarine attack. Thoroughly alarmed, J.W.'s first thought was for his wife, who could not be found on deck; eventually he discovered her and upon being told what all the fuss was about, she calmly remarked that she wondered why all the water suddenly ran to one end of the bath!

During the War J.W. was directed to work of national importance at Keighley, Yorkshire, and he took the opportunity of joining the local cricket club in the company of several other great players of the time, including Frank Woolley and Schofield Haigh the famous Yorkshire County player. J.W.'s best season was in 1917 when he topped the batting with an average of 50.50. The following year Keighley just failed to win the Bradford League Championship,

Saltaire beating them by 3 points. 1919 saw the ground jubilee of the club, and was the most notable season in their history; they won the championship for the first time, and the club membership reached 1,000 for the first time. Herbert Haigh, Woolley and J.W. Hearne led the batting averages, whilst Woolley had top bowling figures.

There is no doubt that the few years before and after the First World War saw J.W. at his very best; at the age of eighteen in 1909 he had made a few appearances in first class matches; by 1910 he had become a regular member of the Middlesex team and by the following year he was one of the top all-round cricketers in the country. It is true to say that in the seasons of 1913, 1914, 1919 and 1920 both J.W. and Woolley were the very best in England. In three of these summers, 1913, 1914 and 1920, J.W. made over 2,000 runs and took over 100 wickets, a record which at that time had only been achieved by W.G. Grace, Wilfred Rhodes, C.L. Townsend, George Hirst and Frank Woolley. In 1920 it was reckoned that only Jack Hobbs was a better batsman. (J.W. was always of the opinion that Hobbs was the best batsman he saw on *any* wicket).

With such a spectacular beginning, his early career outstripped that of his erstwhile companion Patsy Hendren; however, it has to be said that whilst J.W.'s playing powers abated later on, Patsy seemed to go from strength to strength, enjoying a true 'Indian Summer' towards the end of his playing days.

Two more tours, both to Australia, in 1920-21 and 1924-25 were to conclude J.W.'s overseas cricket. The 1920-21 trip was the first one to be undertaken by MCC after the First World War. The Australians had invited them to send out a team the previous winter but this had been declined, and so on 18th September 1920 the team sailed from Tilbury in the R.M.S. *Osterley*, calling at Toulon and Naples and then coaling at Port Said and Colombo, where a one-day match against Ceylon ended in a draw. As a precaution against a seaborne case of typhoid the players had to spend a rather enjoyable week in quarantine in Freemantle and thus missed what would have been an opening four day match at Perth.

Due to severe lumbago during the second Test Match at Melbourne, J.W. did not play again on the tour. With only six matches to his credit he topped the batting averages at 62.00 runs per innings, including 128 against South Australia at Adelaide and 81 versus New South Wales at Sydney.

In 1924 a South African side toured England, playing five Test Matches, drawing two and losing the other three. The fifth Test at the Oval is worthy of note, not because J.W. achieved anything outstanding but because one of the opening batsmen for South Africa was one of his relatives, G.A.L. Hearne, the son of Frank Hearne who had emigrated in 1889.

J.W. on his way to 114 in the Second Test in Australia – 1911/1912.

MIDDLESEX 1920
back (l to r): H.W.Lee, C.H.L.Skeet, F.J.Durston, N.E.Haig, G.T.S.Stevens, H.K.Longman.
front: J.W.Hearne, F.T.Mann, P.F.Warner, H.R.Murrell, E.H.Hendren.

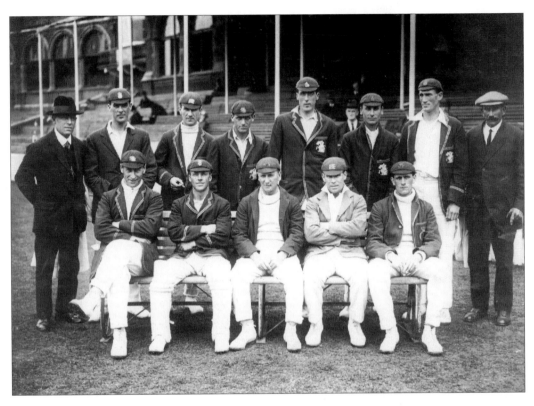

PLAYERS TEAM v GENTLEMEN, THE OVAL, 1919
back (l to r):   A.Kennedy, J.W.Hearne, W.Hitch, F.E.Woolley, J.B.Hobbs, G.Brown
front: C.P.Mead, H.Strudwick, J.T.Tyldesley, E.H.Hendren, C.H.Parkin

1920/21 TOUR

EN ROUTE TO AUSTRALIA
back (l to r): A.C.Russell, E.R.Wilson, F.E.Woolley, C.H.Parkin, A.Waddington, P.G.H.Fender
centre: J.B.Hobbs, E.H.Hendren, J.W.H.T.Douglas, J.W.Hearne, J.W.H.Makepeace
front: H.Howell, A.Dolphin, H.Strudwick

THE FULL SQUAD
back (l to r): A.Dolphin, J.W.Hitch, C.H.Parkin, F.C.Toone(Mgr.), F.E.Woolley, A.C.Russell, A.Waddington
centre: H.Strudwick, W.Rhodes, E.R.Wilson, J.W.H.T.Douglas, P.G.H.Fender, J.B.Hobbs
front: H.Howell, E.H.Hendren, J.W.Hearne, J.W.H.Makepeace

TWICE ONE OF FOUR MIDDLESEX CENTURIONS
IN ONE INNINGS

v SUSSEX 1920
P.F.Warner, H.W.Lee, J.W.Hearne, N.E.Haig

v HAMPSHIRE 1923
H.L.Dales, H.W.Lee, J.W.Hearne, E.H.Hendren

On his last tour in 1924-5, J.W. was only moderately successful, his best match being against Victoria at Melbourne when he scored 193 and took 5 for 30, MCC winning by an innings and 271 runs.

This will be a convenient place to pause for a moment and consider the effect that a professional cricketer's tours had on his family in those far-off days.

The departure from England usually took place in September, and the men did not see their families again until early the following spring, usually in April. Thus, wives had to manage their households and look after the children for over six months of the year on their own, during the worst seasons of the year. Communication was sparse; an ordinary letter, being the regular means of contact, took a long time to arrive, and in the event of an emergency precise details were hard to come by and could cause extreme strain and anxiety. Young children naturally found it impossible to comprehend why their father was going away for such long periods, and although they would be accustomed to short partings during away matches in the summer, a whole winter without him was a traumatic experience. For those slightly older boys such as J.W.'s sons it meant no more fishing and shooting expeditions, no more hilarious interludes with 'Uncle' Patsy Hendren or visits from dear old 'Uncle' Joe Murrell with his gifts of foreign stamps; so it was a rather empty and bleak prospect for half a year which even Christmas did not make up for.

J.W.'s wife Violet Mary was lucky in one respect, as her husband's parents lived a short distance away in Harlington village, whilst her own supportive family were not much further distant at Dawley.

Perhaps the tours also took a toll on John William for he never again achieved the peak form that he enjoyed in 1920. This is not to say that he failed to achieve exceptional feats in later years, as an examination of his match figures shows. For instance, in 1923 he scored over 1,500 runs with an average of 50 and had also taken 113 wickets by the middle of July when illness laid him low for the remainder of the season. The next few years show a decline in his record, although in 1928 he was playing in great form again, and towards the end of June he was fourth in the averages when he was so severely injured that he did not play again that summer. He was still good enough to make the highest score of his career in 1929, with 285 not out against Essex, then a record score for the County.

It has been said that ill-health had a very adverse effect on J.W.'s career, so much so that it would be easy to gain the impression that he was at times a semi-invalid struggling to carry on his game against all odds. Of course he did suffer more than his share of sickness, and when he was laid low this often occurred at significant times which served to highlight his incapacity. Another factor which might encourage this false impression could be early photographs of him which often show what appears to be a frail and drawn individual. To contrast such pictures with the one on page 154, depicting J.W. going in to bat with G.O. Allen, might help to dispel such an impression. In any event, he spent all his active life in vigorous outdoor pursuits and lived to be 74 years old, and even towards the end of his life he still enjoyed his gardening.

Once or twice broken finger-bones resulted in periods of enforced in-activity. These broken bones were not always the consequence of balls which behaved unexpectedly whilst he was batting, and some writers, seeking to exaggerate such things even in those days, have suggested that he had brittle bones. The worst injury of this sort that he received was in June 1928 when Middlesex were playing the West Indies at Lord's. Learie Constantine, playing back to a ball from J.W., hit the ball so hard that after hitting the pavilion rails it damaged woodwork and paint and scattered startled members all over the place, this after striking the bowler's fingers on the way. Brittle bones, indeed! Receiving sympathy and praise for having had the courage to attempt to catch such a ferocious drive, J.W. replied in his usual laconic manner that bravery had nothing to do with it, adding that it was a darn silly try at the impossible.

Cricket writers all agree that John William was always impeccably turned out on the field. He abhorred a sloppily attired player, and the following little incident illustrates his attitude perfectly. One of his sons learnt that his father was coming to watch him play in a local club match, so pads were cleaned, boots whitened and even the marks of edged balls were carefully removed from the face of his bat. In due course the young man presented himself to his father, trousers neatly creased, pad straps correctly tucked away, apparently a model of a well dressed cricketer with the proud news that he was to open the innings. Calm parental eyes examined this snow-white vision, then came the remark, "We all know you will never become an England opener, my son, but there's no reason why you shouldn't look like one. For goodness' sake, make sure both your sleeves are rolled up to match".

Neither of J.W.'s sons displayed the talent nor any great desire to become a cricketer, and their father did not influence them otherwise. Like all the other cricketing fathers of his family, he always felt that unless a lad showed exceptional aptitude then an alternative means of employment was essential, and even the best should have something to fall back on if their career should unfortunately be terminated by injury or illness. No doubt his own experiences were responsible for this attitude. He was, however, only too willing to offer advice and a spot of coaching, and he also enjoyed watching the boys playing school and club cricket.

During his long career, J.W. featured in numerous records with bat and ball. Among those which gave him most pleasure were two occasions when he, along with the other first three Middlesex batsmen, all scored centuries. The initial occasion was at Lord's against Sussex on 22nd and 24th May 1920 when the Middlesex innings was as follows:-

P.F. Warner c Street b Gilligan	139
H.W. Lee c Roberts b Gilligan	119
J.W. Hearne not out	116
N. Haig c H.L. Wilson b Tate	131
Hendren c Gilligan b Tate	17
Extras	21
	543 – 4 wkts. declared

This was a new county cricket record, to be repeated in 1923, this time against Hampshire at Southampton when J.W. made 232, his partners being H.W. Lee, H.L. Dales, and Hendren.

Special bowling feats used to result in the gift from the County of the ball encircled with a silver band engraved with details of the exploit. Although J.W. was never a trophy collector he did nevertheless look forward to the receipt of these balls, which over the course of years became quite numerous.

Technique and timing were the features of John William's batting style, a perfectly-timed single along the ground, splitting a carefully packed area of the field gave far more satisfaction than a bludgeoned six; if a boundary resulted, then so much the better. The impression may have been given that he was not a hard driver of the ball, but here again, timing and a masterly style could be deceptive as many a rueful fieldsman found to his cost as the ball sped past him. With the straightest of bats he could present an impregnable defence particularly when playing on really bad batting wickets. He will probably be remembered for his skill in forcing the ball off his back foot between cover point and point in a manner of his own, and he often played well outside the off stump. Nigel Haig wrote:- "Of all the great batsmen I have seen, J.W. Hearne was the farthest removed from showmanship . . . he had a wit whose depth and breadth embraced many people and most things."

Many of his admirers used to wonder why J.W. bowled so frequently from the pavilion end at Lord's. There were two reasons: the first, not so apparent, was because he felt the pavilion background loomed so close and dark, making it difficult to strike a length, whereas bowling toward the more open nursery end overcame this problem. The more significant reason lay in the cross fall of the pitch, so that, when he was really turning his wrist over and bowling googlies, this slope materially assisted the 'wrong 'un', especially before he broke his wrist whilst roller skating.

His run up to the wicket, if it can be so described, consisted of five or six short quick steps with his arm coming over in what has been called a 'whirling action', the ball being delivered at anything but a slow pace, with the googly as an alternative to a really vicious leg break. Later in his career the off break became his main weapon.

J.W. had an imperturbable temperament and was not often given to much outward expression, either on or off the field. One day, whilst batting against the fast bowling of A.E.R. Gilligan and with Middlesex facing defeat, he played and missed a well pitched up straight ball which struck him fair and square on the big toe. Conscious that he would certainly be given out lbw if the bowler appealed he somehow stifled the pain, his face remaining inscrutable. Gilligan glared down the pitch for what seemed an interminable period, before eventually asking the umpire for his sweater and 'over' was called. The bowler at the other end commenced his run, whereupon J.W. expressed his agony in no uncertain terms, and Gilligan commented, "Jack, you old devil, you didn't play my last ball, did you?" The batsman's reply is unprintable but one wonders what he would have done if his team's situation had not been so critical.

In a more serious vein, he was visibly moved when he returned home from Finchley Crematorium after attending the funeral of Patsy Hendren. In fact, only the death of his younger son, killed early in the Second World War whilst flying with the R.A.F., visibly affected him more.

At the end of his playing career he arrived home one day clearly in an angry mood. Upon being questioned as to what had upset him so much, he replied that there was a very promising young player who had been foolish enough to become involved in a car accident; "silly young boy, he might even be good enough to play for England, and there he is trying to break his neck." The young man in question was D.C.S. Compton. The thought that so much latent talent could be put at risk was just too much for John William to bear.

Friendships abounded, especially during the inter-war years, cemented by the closeness of long periods together on overseas tours where tensions on

PLAYERS TEAM v. GENTLEMEN AT SCARBOROUGH, 1921
back (l to r): J.W.Hitch, W.Rhodes, F.E.Woolley, G.Brown, A.S.Kennedy, A.Sandham
front: J.W.Hearne, E.H.Hendren, G.H.Hirst, P.Holmes, C.P.Mead

COACHING AT CAMBRIDGE, 1921
J.W. with C.T.Ashton, A.P.F.Chapman, G.O.Shelmerdine

ENGLAND TEAM TO AUSTRALIA 1924-25
back (l to r): R.Tyldesley (inset), H.Howell, E.H.Hendren, M.W.Tate, R.Kilner, J.L.Bryan
centre: F.C.Toone (mgr.), A.Sandham, W.Whysall, A.P.F.Chapman, J.W.Hearne
H.Sutcliffe, A.P.Freeman
front: F.E.Woolley, J.W.H.T.Douglas, A.E.R.Gilligan, J.B.Hobbs, H.Strudwick

With Jack Hobbs and friend on an earlier tour.

and off the field could strain the strongest bonds of comradeship. Patsy Hendren was, needless to say, his closest companion. Patsy, the perfect extroverted complement to J.W.'s quiet manner of deflecting the limelight, was a great favourite of the latter's two sons, and having no children of his own he delighted in the boys' company, recounting comic stories and pulling their legs unmercifully.

J.W. and E.J. 'Tiger' Smith, the Warwickshire wicket keeper, formed a close friendship over very many years. When Warwickshire were playing at Lord's 'Tiger' would stay at J.W.'s home; likewise, J.W. would live with the Smiths when Middlesex were playing at Edgbaston. On one such visit both wives and their children went to the match, an occasion remembered with some embarrassment for, with Middlesex in the field and J.W. positioned fairly close to the boundary, his youngest son, then only a toddler, somehow escaped from his mother's care and ran on to the ground, making a beeline for his father. Naturally this amused the crowd but not J.W. who, for once, was at a loss to know how to cope!

Harry Lee, Andrew Sandham and Maurice Tate were others among a host of close friends of long standing. Mention must also be made of Jim Smith, the Middlesex fast bowler. Jim was by any standard a big man; J.W.'s wife said that his smile alone was large enough to fill her small living room. He had become fascinated by J.W.'s droll fishing yarns, and expressed a wish to be taken on an outing as he felt that, although J.W. had failed to teach him how to bat in the classic manner, he might do better as a fishing instructor! So off they went in a boat on a large lake which contained a good stock of fish. Of course, like all good fishing stories, it goes without saying that whilst J.W. hauled in a good catch on one side, there seemed a singular lack of fish on his partner's side of the boat, so that Jim eventually suggested a change-over. Not much imagination is needed to visualise the ensuing pantomime as the giant and his companion swapped places in their small craft.

In 1922 J.W. took over the running of the sports shop at 137 Uxbridge Road, West Ealing, or 'MCC House' as it had been named by 'Old Tom' many years earlier. Up until that date the business had been continued by Tom's widow Caroline Ann. For a few years one of J.W.'s cousins, Frederick Sabin, acted as manager, but when he left to join the sports department of a large London store in 1926 J.W. was at a loss to replace him. However, good fortune was at hand in the shape of Leonard Philip Flick. Born in 1903, 'Len', as he was popularly known, had been acquainted with J.W. through their membership of Norwood Green Cricket Club, and a chance remark led to him becoming the manager and co-director of the new J.W. Hearne Ltd.

Numerous sporting folk and clubs will remember with affection Len's skill at repairing their sports equipment. He was assisted in this activity by Harold Skarin for over forty years. Harold's death in 1973 resulted in the decision to close the business early in 1974, so Len Flick did not quite complete half a century at the shop which Tom Hearne had set up over a hundred years earlier.

John William coached at King's College School, Wimbledon for a while in the late 1930's, and early in World War II he joined the War Reserve Constabulary before taking over the *Bricklayers Arms* on the northern side of the Bath Road, Harlington, later directly opposite London Airport, and which was subsequently renamed the *Air Hostess*. It has now been demolished together with most of the pre-war property to make way for the ever-advancing tide of commercial development.

Soon after the War J.W. 'retired' to live at Bagley Close, West Drayton, but cricket had not finished with him, for he was delighted to accept an invitation to become coach/scout for Middlesex County Cricket Club, having first suggested that there was a need to improve the grass-roots of Middlesex cricket. At about the same time he coached at Westminster School and Latimer School in 1951.

The next five years, April 1953 to August 1958, were among the happiest of his life and, together with Jim Sims, he saw the development of several promising young players, some of whom were destined to become County and England players. Advice and encouragement for men new to the world of first class cricket were freely given by J.W.; he remembered only too well his own introduction to the game. The late Sir George (Gubby) Allen and Denis Compton, among others, have confirmed the help they received from him in their early days.

Another Middlesex amateur who struck up a close friendship with J.W. was Greville (G.T.S.) Stevens. He was always a great favourite of the author, having presented him with a beautiful model sailing ship at Lord's which proved much more interesting to a small boy than the cricket match then going on, and he is remembered with affection.

John Murray, the brilliant Middlesex and England wicket keeper, particularly had much to thank J.W. for. Coming from a humble background and not long out of school, Murray initially had a great feeling of insecurity in the awe-inspiring surroundings of Lord's. The words of J.W. to him were characteristically few but as usual very much to the point, so much so that from then on the young man felt that he had found someone who really cared. When Murray was playing his first couple of games for the County First XI,

*R.E.S.Wyatt and J.W.Hearne going out to bat for an
England XI v Australians at Folkstone, 1930.*

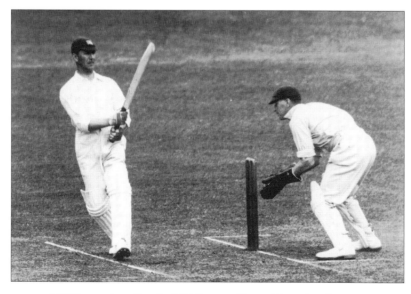

*J.W.Hearne in action for Middlesex v Hampshire at Lords, 1927
when he scored 121.*

G.O.Allen and J.W.Hearne going out to bat for
Middlesex v Nottinghamshire at Lords, 1926.
(J.W.'s favourite photo.)

Middlesex at the nets in 1927 with Durston comparing the new small ball
with the old for the benefit of Price, Lee and J.W.Hearne.

with Leslie Compton unable to keep wicket on account of a bad back, J.W. went to the trouble of persuading Herbert Strudwick, then scoring for Surrey, to turn up early at the next match between the two counties at Lord's in order to give John some personal coaching. Of course "Struddy" readily consented and such caring generosity has never been forgotten.

It is not surprising that there have been close ties between the Hearnes and other families who have served at Lord's cricket ground for many generations. One such family, the Slatters, come readily to mind as William Slatter was a contemporary of George Francis Hearne; they were both among the founder members of the well-known club which became the Cross Arrows Cricket Club. In his time William H. Slatter was engaged on various ground activities and would have known 'old Tom' Hearne and his son Thomas Arthur. William was responsible for the painting and decorating until he became Clerk of the Works in 1904. William's father, well-known as 'Stevey', was first employed by MCC early in the 1830s before the first Hearne appeared there.

Another member of the Lord's staff who was held in great affection by all the Hearnes associated with Lord's was Jimmy Cannon who served there from 1876 for 65 years. He was only 12 years old when he began as the tennis court ball boy, also looking after members' horses. Eventually he became chief clerk and was made an honorary member of MCC when he retired.

The other family with close ties were the Gabys. Old Dick Gaby came to Lord's when he was 15 years old in 1873 and like William Slatter did all manner of jobs, becoming lawn tennis professional and managing the smaller of the score boards. He was also a founder member of the Cross Arrows. When he retired aged 78 he and his son Dick had achieved one hundred years' unbroken service at Lord's between them. In 1929 young Dick started in very junior roles but eventually in 1946 he was appointed Clerk to the then Board of Control for home Test Matches, to the Advisory County Cricket Committee and to the Imperial Cricket Conference. He carried out these roles until the formation of the Test and County Cricket Board in 1967 when he undertook other MCC duties. At his retirement in 1973 he had become Club Superintendent and Staff Manager, a far cry from his initial activities. In appreciation of his services, both MCC and Middlesex CCC bestowed upon him Honorary Life Membership of their respective clubs. His elder brother G.M. Gaby, better known as 'Joe', was employed at Lord's, during the cricket seasons only, from 1921 until his death in 1975, a total of 54 years' loyal service.

When John William eventually discontinued his activities with Middlesex

"Left elbow up"
J.W. coaching in later life.

Sir Pelham Warner presenting retirement tankards to J.W. Hearne and E. Hendren
at the Middlesex AGM, 1938.

CCC he spent the remaining few years of his life pottering in his garden and critically viewing televised cricket. Only a few days after having a few friends at home to watch the last match of the season, an England XI versus The Rest of the World XI, he fell into a coma and died on the morning of 13th September 1965 as quietly as he had played all his long and eventful life.

Chapter 15

William Hearn(e)
(MCC 1878-91)

O N THE face of it the life of William Hearn would appear to be devoid of complications for the family researcher, even allowing for the spelling of his name as recounted by George Francis Hearne.

There is almost no doubt that he was related to the main branch of the family cricketers, and that George Francis was correct in his assertion that William was "one of us" Definitely accepted as 'family', it is certain that he would not have been included in the Hearne XI if the case had been otherwise. There were numerous other young relatives, equally good players, who could easily have been chosen if his uncles and cousins had thought he did not qualify. It is also significant that a number of members of the Hearne family attended his funeral.

William was born at Essendon on 13th November 1849. Essendon is a quiet little village in Hertfordshire, situated a short distance to the east of Hatfield House, on a hill overlooking the valley of the River Lea. It has not changed very much since William lived there and many parts now look as they did in the second part of the nineteenth century. William's parents were James Hearn and Sarah, formerly Pearce. James's occupation is given as a grocer on the birth certificate. James and Sarah had been married at Rickmansworth Church on 29th June 1840, at which time James was a cordwainer or shoemaker, and Sarah's father, William Pearce, was a baker. James's father is shown on the marriage certificate as a farmer born in Great Missenden, whilst his wife Sarah, also a grocer, was born in Sandridge.

James and Sarah died at Cheshunt, in 1894 and 1899 respectively, but in view of their close association with Essendon they were buried there.

So far, so good! It is when William's grandparents are sought that questions can be raised, for it would appear that his grandmother, Martha Hearn of Barley Mow Lane, Great Missenden, gave birth to a son on 27th February 1815 who was baptised James Ives Hearn on 9th April 1815, shown 'baseborn' in the Parish Register. It can reasonably be assumed that 'Ives' was the father's surname; if this was the case and James Ives Hearn was in fact William's father, then the reason for the reticence and the various stories concerning his family's past becomes plain. Births out of wedlock were more reprehensible then than now.

W.Hearne

William was a shoemaker by trade who, whilst an excellent cricketer, will always be remembered as one of the best-known umpires of his era; he was a very good batsman, with a modest opinion of his own round arm bowling, and a fine cover point with a superb return to the wicket. Whilst playing at Essendon he was spotted by V.E. Walker, who suggested that he should go on to Lord's. William was not so sure that his ability was sufficient, especially as a bowler, but Walker pointed out that men who could bat and field were sometimes required, so, in 1878, he was engaged by MCC and remained in their employment until the day he died.

William's first match at Lord's was on 12th May 1870 playing for Hertfordshire *v* MCC. He was bowled by Shaw in the first innings for 10, and in the second innings caught and bowled by the same bowler for 4. In the same match Tom Hearne took 3 for 27 and 4 for 26 for MCC. Rain stopped play at a crucial point in the match when Hertfordshire had scored 50 and 79 and MCC had replied with 53 and 39 for 3.

William played regularly for Essendon from the age of 14 onwards, and was engaged by the St. Alban's Cricket Club in 1870. He also made frequent appearances for MCC and Ground, often in or against distinguished company.

William's highest score of 167 was for Hertfordshire in 1887 against MCC at Lord's. For MCC and Ground he made 177 not out versus Notts Castle, 160 against Uppingham Rovers and 149 against Suffolk. He had as his benefit the match at Watford in August 1893 between Hertfordshire and Bedfordshire, and in 1897 he received the proceeds of the Middlesex *v* Somerset match at Lord's from MCC as a reward for his services.

William Hearn(e) died rather suddenly at Barnet on 30th January 1904. He was a popular man and was greatly missed by all his friends and acquaintances. His obituary in *Wisden* states: "He was buried in the Christ Church Cemetery, High Barnet, on February 4th, several prominent cricketers including Mr. Henry Perkins, George Burton, J.T., G.F. and G.G. Hearne being present. At the conclusion of the burial service Canon Trotter, an Old Harrovian and a keen devotee of the game, referred to the prestige the deceased has gained as a cricketer and umpire, and spoke in laudatory terms of cricket as a game".

Chapter 16

Some William Hearnes

NO DOUBT the reader has, from time to time, been confused by the repetitive Christian names among the Hearne family. The author too soon discovered that the lack of a second name in those early times was a severe handicap to research.

In order to clarify the position relating to the several William Hearnes known to be active cricketers, it is hoped that the following notes will prove useful.

WILLIAM, 1797, wheelwright   of Chalfont St. Peter, married Catharine from Scotland. There are no records of his participation in the game but undoubtedly he did play club cricket, for his grandson John Herbert passed on mentions of William and of his father, John, to the author. This particular William is the only variant in a direct line of John Hearnes from the early 1700's to the present day.

WILLIAM, 1828 - 1908, builder and undertaker,   married Mary Montague. Probably best known as the father of the three of his sons who became first class professional players – Herbert, Walter and John Thomas. He was a nephew of William the wheelwright and might have attained some fame had he devoted more attention to the game. During the 1840's he became one of the best cricketers in South Buckinghamshire, and made many large scores for the Chalfont St. Giles village club. He was a hard hitter of the ball with a fine straight drive and square cut. He continued to make good scores until he was nearly fifty years of age, after which he still took a good interest in the game until eventually a stroke rendered him partially paralysed.

WILLIAM HEARN(E), 1849 - 1904,   best known for his fame as a first class umpire, he was also an excellent player. His immediate family and his career are the subject of chapter 15.

WILLIAM, 1860 - 1916,   married Rebecca Dunkley, Chalfont St. Giles. The younger brother of Herbert, Walter and John Thomas, he was another of the numerous Hearnes who, although fine players, did not achieve first class status. He was groundsman for the Household Brigade Cricket Club from 1887 to 1898 after which he went to Wellington College as coach and groundsman for sixteen years. He regularly played at Canterbury in an annual match arranged by his brother Walter and he usually made a good score. During the summer terms of 1914 and 1915 he was employed as bowler at Winchester College. In November 1916, whilst working as assistant storekeeper for Graysons, ship repairers of Liverpool, he was killed when cylinders of acetylene exploded while being unloaded. His three sons were all very good cricketers.

Chapter 17

The Family

THE cricketing Hearnes were predominantly all-rounders. In style and method of play, whether bowling or batting, they had their own individual characteristics.

Collectively, their bowling encompassed the whole range of styles from old-time underhand and round arm to the overarm fast, medium and slow of a later era.

The same could be said of their batting, from those whose main object was to hit the ball as hard as possible without too much regard for the niceties of defence to the skill and artistry of J.W. 'Old Tom', for example, was not noted for defensive play but he was far from being just a slogger (he was one of the last to exploit the old-fashioned 'draw'). Years later, J.W.'s defensive technique made him a very difficult batsman to dismiss, yet, at the height of his career, he ranked as one of the most entertaining of stroke players.

Most of the Hearnes were at least good fielders, and Frank in particular was described as brilliant, whilst J.W. was known to have a safe pair of hands, especially in his younger days.

However, from all this varied talent, none kept wicket as a specialist, although I fancy "Old Tom" might have had something to say about this!

All-round ability applied equally to those of the family who played the game professionally without attaining first-class status. While keenness to play a full part in the game no doubt contributed, probably a more practical reason may have been that a professional had a better chance of being engaged, particularly in the early days if he had more than one string to his bow; for the same reason a number became groundsmen and acted as umpires later in life.

Physically, the cricketing Hearnes have nearly all been tall, lean men, a characteristic of the family to this day. Prominent exceptions were the Kent trio, each of whom was small, and it is noticeable that Alec appears at the foot of most team and group photographs, as though self-conscious of his lack of inches.

All, in the best sense, were good men who enjoyed the respect of their contemporaries within and outside the game. They were men with a respect for authority, who were prepared to give of their best and rightly expected fair treatment in return. To a large extent, this expectation was justified.

Typically, they were home-loving men with great affection for their families and, by extension, for each other. None intentionally sought the limelight, although they were justly proud of their achievements, and most could be described as self-effacing.

Possibly the most extrovert was 'Old George' with his penchant for telling outrageous stories, but each had his own sense of humour, including J.W. whose composed expression could so disguise a good "leg-pull" that even his sons were taken in more often than not!

Dual threads of artistic talent and a love of nature were evident in among others Frank, J.T. and J.W., and these interests have re-emerged in the present generation.

When I speculate on what my forebears were like, I would say without much hesitation that these studies have revealed they were not markedly different from their descendants. All the present-day members of the family are endowed with many of the same characteristics as the cricketers, both physically and in other ways, and I have no reason to doubt that the attributes and characteristics of the Hearnes of former years will be carried forward into future generations.

Acknowledgements

My grateful thanks to the kind people mentioned in the text and to all the following who have so generously given their time and effort:-

The late Leslie Ames; Robert Brooke; Dr Ali Bacher; Wilf Broughton; Derek Carlaw; David Frith; Christopher Martin-Jenkins; Hayward Kidson; David Lemmon; T. Osborn; Richard Parkins; Netta Rheinberg; the late Peter Sichel; Kent County Cricket Club; Middlesex County Cricket Club; The Secretary of M.C.C.; Stephen Green, Curator of the M.C.C. library & museum and his staff; The Association of Cricket Statisticians; The Local History & Local Studies Librarians of the following Public Libraries – Aylesbury, Canterbury, Ealing, Enfield, Hounslow, Lewisham, Rickmansworth, Uxbridge.

Special thanks are due to Anita Ellis, Joan Graves, Penelope Leggett and Elaine Tapley who typed the manuscript, and to my lifelong friend Eric Wood who undertook numerous researches into his Wisdens on my behalf. To Gerald Clarke of Photocare, Kingham, Oxon who so expertly cleaned, repaired and reproduced so many family illustrations. I am also indebted to E.W. Swanton who has contributed a worthy Foreword and to Tony Laughton and Michael Down at Boundary Books for bringing the book to publication.

Finally to my wife, who so patiently assisted and supported me in this undertaking, I express my undying gratitude.

J.W. Hearne
Hillingdon, January 1996

Statistical Appendix

Hearne Family
Individual first class career records

BATTING AND FIELDING

		Matches	Innings	Not out	Runs	Highest score	Average	Hundreds	Caught	Stumped
Alec	All	488	833	78	16436	194	21.65	15	404	0
	Test	1	1	0	9	9	9.00	0	1	0
Frank	All	161	285	20	4760	144	17.96	4	111	0
	Test	6	10	0	168	30	16.80	0	3	0
George	All	20	32	6	550	72	21.15	0	15	2
George A.L.	All	41	72	2	1981	138	28.30	2	38	2
	Test	3	5	0	59	28	11.80	0	3	0
George F.	All	1	1	0	26	26	26.00	0	0	0
George G.	All	328	571	56	9022	126	17.51	5	214	0
	Test	1	1	0	0	0	0.00	0	0	0
Herbert	All	25	36	9	252	36	9.33	0	16	0
John T.	All	639	919	318	7205	71	11.98	0	426	0
	Test	12	18	4	126	40	9.00	0	4	0
John W.	All	647	1025	116	37252	285 *	40.98	96	348	0
	Test	24	36	5	806	114	26.00	1	13	0
Thomas	All	173	292	20	5048	146	18.55	4	116	7
Thomas J.	All	1	–	–	–	–	–	–	0	0
Walter	All	55	92	19	553	34 *	7.57	0	23	0
William	All	41	72	5	806	91	12.02	0	27	0

* Not out

Hearne Family
Individual first class career records

BOWLING

		Runs	Wickets	Average	5 wickets in innings	10 wickets in match	Best
Alec	All	23120	1160	19.93	52	9	8 - 15
Frank	All	1346	57	23.61	1	0	5 - 47
	Test	40	2	20.00	0	0	2 - 40
George A.L.	All	401	14	28.64	0	0	3 - 9
George F.	All	23	0	–	0	0	–
George G.	All	11503	686	16.76	41	12	8.21
Herbert	All	1415	57	24.82	3	0	5.27
John T.	All	54352	3061	17.75	255	66	9.32
	Test	1082	49	22.08	4	1	6.41
John W.	All	44926	1839	24.42	107	23	9.61
	Test	1462	30	48.73	1	0	5.49
Thomas	All	3994	283 *	14.11	16	2	6.12
Walter	All	4349	273	15.93	28	10	8.40
William	All	57	0	–	0	0	–

* Plus 9 wickets taken, bowling analysis not extant

These statistics are extracted from the 1993 edition of *Who's Who of Cricketers* by Philip Bailey, Philip Thorn and Peter Wynne-Thomas, published by Hamlyn and the Association of Cricket Statisticians, and are gratefully acknowledged.

Index

Abel, R.   43, 76, 120
Absolom, C.A.   62
Absolon, C.   50, 51, 56
Aikman, Col. R.   97, 98
Allen, Sir G.O.B.   131, 146, 152
Atkins, F.M.   87
Attewell, W.   67

Balaskas, X.C.   80
Baldwin, Mrs. S.   130
Barbour, T.C.   97
Bendall, I.   106
Benn, J.   135
Bettesworth, W.A.   45, 110
Bevan, Hon. Mrs.   130
Biddulph, S.   57
Blythe, C.   93
Bosanquet, B.J.T.   126
Bowyer, Col. W.J.   129
Brack, A.   96
Briggs, J.   76
Brockwell, W.   78, 121, 129
Brough, L.   107
Broughton, W.   14
Brown, J.T.   123
Bruce, Mr.   43
Brune, C.J.   33
Brunshill, H.F.   67
Budden, G.   105
Burnup, C.J.   93, 94
Burton, D.   44
Burton, F. (Jnr.)   44
Burton, F. (Snr.)   44, 107
Burton, G.   160

Cannon, J.   155
Cantelupe, Viscount   80, 89
Carpenter, R.P.   21
Case, T.   23, 25, 50, 53
Catling, W.   53
Cazalet, P.Y.F.   117
Champain, F.H.B.   92
Christopherson, S.   65
Clarke, W.   19, 20
Clayton, R.D.   41
Clilverd, J.   12
Collins, W.E.W.   118
Compton, D.C.S.   138, 148, 152
Compton, L.H.   155
Constantine, Lord L.H. 146
Cooper, B.B.   51, 53

Coppinger, S.   50
Cornwallis, Capt. W.S. 12
Cox, G.R.   89
Crossland, J.   64
Crow, –   111
Cunningham, Capt. B.   97, 98
Currie, Sir D.   79

Dales, H.L.   147
Dark, J.H.   40, 41
Dark, S.   38
Day, H.   33
Dean, J.   56
Dixon, J.A.   119
Douglas, J.W.H.T.   138
Druitt, M.J.   65
Dutnall, F.   114
Dutnall, W.M.   114

East, R.W.   46
Edwards, M.   53
Eglinton, Lord   96, 97, 98
Eve, G.   88

Fagg, A.   114, 115
Fagg, E.   114
Fagg, J.   114
Fagg, L.   114, 131
Fellows, H.W.   12, 14, 15, 17, 19, 32
Fennell, J.   39
Ferris, J.J.   79
Ferryman, E.   114
Findley, G.   98
Finnie, J.   98
Firkin, –.   78
Fitzgerald, R.A.   39, 40
Flick, L.P.   151, 152
Flowers, W.   111, 119
Ford, Mr.   43
Ford, Mr.   117
Fothergill, A.J.   76
Fry, C.B.   120

Gaby, G.M.   155
Gaby, R. (Jnr.)   38, 39, 155
Gaby, R. (Snr.)   39, 155
Garrard, H.   129
Giffen, G.   123
Gilligan, A.E.R.   148
Gonzalez, P.   109
Gordon, N.   107

Grace, E.M.	25, 31, 119	Hearne, Frank (Cousin)	8
Grace, W.G.	14, 31, 33, 43, 62, 63, 69, 80	Hearne, Frank V.A.	80, 100
	81, 88, 89, 119, 120, 124, 140	Hearne, George	11, 18, 19, 23, 25, 28, 34
Gregory, S.E.	123		44, 49-60, 64, 68-71, 85
Gregson, –.	98		105, 164
Grimston, Hon. R.	40	Hearne, George A.L.	8, 80, 100-104, 140
Grundy, J.	26, 51	Hearne, George F.	33, 37-46, 65, 155, 158
Gunn, W.	124, 131		160
Gurney, W.	42	Hearne, George G.	33, 42, 45, 48-50, 55
			59-74, 77, 79, 87-89
Haig, N.E.	147		110, 111, 121, 160
Haigh, H.	140	Hearne, George W.	81, 82, 100, 103
Haigh, S.	139	Hearne, Gladys	88
Hale, H.	12	Hearne, Hannah	12
Halliwell, E.A.	80	Hearne, (Fagg), Hannah E.	114
Hamilton, –.	98	Hearne, Harry	8
Hammond, W.R.	107	Hearne (Archer), Hazel	100
Hampden, Viscount	131	Hearne, Henry	105, 116
Harris, Lord	14, 56, 60, 63, 64, 65, 67, 68	Hearne, Henry W.	114
	71, 77, 78, 85, 87, 114	Hearne, Herbert	64, 65, 71, 87, 105-107
Hawke, Lord	80		116, 132, 161
Hay, A.	43	Hearne, James	50
Hay, G.	32, 34	Hearne, John	11, 161
Hayward, T.W.	120	Hearne, John H.	7, 11, 133, 135, 151
Hearn, James I.	158	Hearne, John T.	44, 45, 56, 67, 76, 79, 88
Hearn, Martha	158		89, 105, 106, 114-132
Hearn (Pearce), Sarah	158		135, 139, 160, 161, 164
Hearn(e), William	42, 44, 123, 158-161	Hearne, John William	7, 28, 30, 126, 127, 129
Hearne, Ada M.	65		133-157, 163, 164
Hearne, Alec	7, 41, 42, 45, 55, 64-68, 71, 80	Hearne, John Woodville	103
	81, 83, 85-95, 105, 110, 163	Hearne, Joseph	42, 105, 116
Hearne, Alex E.V.	81, 100	Hearne, Joseph *(1794)*	116
Hearne, Alexander L.	81	Hearne, Kate E.	135
Hearne (Budden), Annie	105, 131	Hearne, Kate M.	25, 99
Hearne, Barrie	48	Hearne (Wakefield), Lavinia E.	28, 99
Hearne (Gregory), Blanche	96, 99	Hearne, Lionel F.	81
Hearne (Newton), Caroline	25, 26, 151	Hearne, Mabel	69
Hearne, Catherine	161	Hearne, Mary A.	105
Hearne (Clilverd), Charlotte	12, 25	Hearne (Gibbons), Mary	50
Hearne, David	40	Hearne (Montague), Mary	105, 161
Hearne, David B.	46, 48	Hearne (Bendall), Mary A.	106
Hearne, (Duffy), Doreen	100	Hearne (Day), Mary A.	33, 35
Hearne, Doris	88	Hearne (Sharon), Mary J.	64, 69
Hearne (Bowyer), Edith A.	129, 130	Hearne, Neil W.	100, 103
Hearne (East), Edith F.	46	Hearne, Phyllis	88, 95
Hearne (Sturgess), Edith M.	106	Hearne, Randolph	50, 54, 83, 96-99
Hearne (Bridgeman), Eliza	33, 37, 44, 46	Hearne, Raymond G.	76, 80-82, 103
Hearne, Elizabeth	11	Hearne (Dunkley), Rebecca	161
Hearne (Eve), Elizabeth R.	88	Hearne (Howes), Rosa L.	71, 80-82, 100
Hearne, Ethel	114, 131	Hearne, Rose M.	49
Hearne, Eustace	88	Hearne (Richardson), Rosina	133, 135
Hearne, F.	44	Hearne (Stevens), Ruby W.	100, 103
Hearne, Frank	8, 49, 55, 59, 64, 65, 67, 69-85	Hearne, Susannah	13, 50
	87, 88, 100-105, 110, 121,	Hearne, T.B.	85
	140, 163, 164	Hearne, Thomas *(1415)*	9

Hearne, Thomas *(1806)*	11, 12	Lowther, Rt. Hon.	136
Hearne, Thomas *(1826)*	11, 12, 14, 15, 17-34, 37	Luckin, M.W.	89
	39-41, 49, 51, 53, 56-59		
	68, 99, 151, 155, 160, 163	Mackinnon, F.A.	67, 77
Hearne, Thomas A.	11, 33-35, 37, 41, 135, 155	Mann, R.	7
Hearne, Thomas J.	37, 45-48, 126	Marchant, D.	7
Hearne (Benn), Violet M.	135, 145, 151	Marchant, F.	111
Hearne, Walter	7, 65, 87, 89, 91, 95, 105	Marsham, G.	67
	111-116, 131, 161	Martin, F.	64, 87, 89, 92
Hearne, William *(1797)*	11, 161	Martin-Jenkins C.	7
Hearne, William *(1828)*	105, 116, 161	Mason, J.R.	89, 91, 92
Hearne, William *(1860)*	105, 116, 118, 161, 162	Mildmay, Lord	117
Henderson, R.	42	Mills, C.H.	78
Hendren, E.H.	33, 126, 127, 140, 145, 147	Mills, Hon. C.T.	136
	148, 151	Mills, G.	40
Hendren J.	136	Milton, J.	117
Hewitt, A.	35	Minto, –.	98
Heyward, S.	135	Montgomerie, Lord	97
Hill, C.	123	Murdoch, J.A.	38, 39
Hilton, P.	85	Murdoch, W.L.	43
Hine-Haycock, Rev. T.R.	43	Murray, J.T.	152, 155
Hirst, G.H.	140	Murrell, H.R.	126, 145
Hoare, Miss	130	Mycroft, W.	41
Hoare, Sir S., Bt	55		
Hobbs, Sir J.B.	138	Nash, G.	64
Hood, Hon. S.	130	Need, P.	39
Hornby, A.N.	105	Newham, W.	41
Howat, G.	77	Newman, A.	135
Howes, W.	71	Newton, J.	25
Hughes, T.B.	118	Nicholson, J.W.F.	95
Huish, F.H.	92, 93	Noble, M.A.	123
Humphreys, G.T.	41	Norris, T.	51, 54
Humphreys, W.A.	41	Nourse, A.W.	101
Hunt, J.H.S.	125		
Hurn, J. atte	9	Ogilvy, A.	130
Hurne, H. en le	9	O'Shaugnessy, E.	64
Hutchings K.L.	94		
		Parker, A.C.	8
Jackson, J.	31	Parr, G.	20, 21, 28
Jessop, G.L.	92	Paterson, Mr.	98
		Patiala, H.H.B., Maharaja of	121, 138, 139
Kidd, A.	59	Patiala, H.N.R., Maharaja of	106, 121, 129
Killick, H.	41	Patterson, W.H.	67, 91
King, K.	41	Payne, C.	53
Knight, W.H.	50	Pearce, P.	34
		Pearce, W.	158
Lambert, G.	39	Peggs, B.	39
Langridge, W.	130	Penn, A.	63
Lee, H.W.	126, 136, 147, 151	Perkins, H.	40, 43, 50, 160
Leveson-Gower, Miss	130	Pike, S.	8
Lillywhite, F.W.	14	Pilch, F.	14
Lillywhite, J. (Jnr.)	42, 53	Pooley, E.	51
Lockwood, W.	124	Pougher, A.D.	123
Lohmann, G.A.	41	Prothero, E.D.	97
Longmuir, –.	98		

Ramsey, R.   64
Ranjitsinjhi, K.S.   25, 120
Rawlin, J.T.   56, 120, 123
Read, J.M.   74, 78
Read, W.W.   31, 67, 88
Reade, Mr.   43
Register, F.   117
Relf, A.E.   41
Relf, J.   41
Relf, R.R.   41
Rhodes, W.   139
Richardson, A.G.   92
Roberts, –.   28, 29
Robertson, Sir. F.A.   121
Russell, J.S.   41
Rutter, E.   29

Sabin, E.   28
Sabin, F.   151
Sandham, A.   151
Scotton, W.H.   107, 119
Seymour, J.   93
Sharon, J.   64
Shaw, A.   42, 160
Sheffield, Lord   79, 81
Shore, Rev. O.   33
Shrewsbury, A.   42, 60, 81, 119
Sickel, H.   130
Silverthorn, Mr.   83
Sims, J.M.   152
Skarin, H.   152
Slatter, S.   155
Slatter, W.H.   39, 155
Smith, Sir. C.A.   74, 79
Smith, C.I.J.   151
Smith, E.J.   151
Somerset, Miss   130
Southerton, J.   53
Spofforth, F.R.   74
Stephenson, H.H.   21, 31
Stevens, G.T.S.   152
Stewart, H.C.   92
Stoddart, A.E.   124, 129
Strang, E.R.   100
Stratford, A.H.   41
Street, A.E.   98
Street, W.   57, 58
Strudwick, H.   155
Stubberfield, H.   41
Sturgess, E.   8, 106, 107, 109
Sturgess, I.   106, 109
Sturgess, W.H.   106
Summers, S.   107

Tapping, M.   8

Tarrant, F.A.   46, 126, 127, 138
Tate, M.W.   151
Theunissen, N.   76
Thoms, R.   29, 32, 44
Titmus, F.J.   127
Townsend, C.L.   140
Trott, A.E.   46, 56, 123-126
Trott, G.H.S.   118
Trotter, Canon   160
Troughton, Col.   114
Twining, V.   130
Tyldesley, J.T.   120

Ulyett, G.   71

Vansittart, Lord   117
Vintcent, C.H.   76

Wakefield, D.   28
Wakefield, F.R.   28
Walker, H.   17
Walker, I.   17
Walker, I.D.   54, 57
Walker, J.   17, 19, 20, 31, 54
Walker, R.D.   17, 25
Walker, V.E.   17, 28, 54, 60, 159
Ward, T.A.   101
Warner, P.F.   91, 126, 127, 137, 138
Warsop, B.   39
Warton, Maj. R.G.   74, 76, 77, 79, 80
Webbe, A.J.   17, 118, 119
Weigall, G.J.V.   92, 95
Welford, –.   98
Wells, C.M.   125
White, H.E.   35
Willsher, E.   50
Wilson, Bishop C.   65
Winfield, B.   49
Wisden, J.   19, 20, 28, 56
Wood, H.   60, 64, 79, 121
Woods, S.M.J.   43
Woolley, F.E.   94, 139, 140
Wootton, J.   64, 87, 111
Worrall, J.   118
Worsley, G.T.   117
Wright, W.   87, 89, 92

Yacoub, Dr. M.   130